VIEWS FROM A WINDOW SEAT

THOUGHTS ON WRITING AND LIFE

JEANNINE ATKINS

Stone Door Press
P.O. Box 226 Whately MA 01093

www.jeannineatkins.com

cover photo: Jeannine Atkins
author photo: Peter Laird
cover and interior design: Peter Laird

To Peter. Not a word of this could be without you.

Contents

Welcome!

Please help yourself to tea or coffee, and join me on days that often begin with gazing out a window and writing about what I see. While most of the short essays in this book can be read in any order, I organized them around the way my view from a window seat changes with the year. I start with spring and thoughts on beginning a book, then move into summer and writing the long middle. During the fall, I focus on the rounds of revision. In winter, I consider the pleasures and anxiety of finishing one book while gathering ideas or images for the next one.

Seasons and phases of writing both have blurry edges. My thoughts on poems and novels sometimes spill rather than stop, and overlap with concerns beyond my laptop. While this book began as blog entries kept over several years, I cut sections, expanded others, and compressed time. Feel free to begin anywhere. And keep a notebook nearby.

Jeannine

Jeannine Atkins

Spring: Beginning

Here in Western Massachusetts, we're apt to raise our eyebrows when reminded that spring is supposed to take up a quarter of the year. Still, we appreciate the change from white to brown to green, no matter the calendar. This hopeful season seems a good time to consider the beginnings of new books. The first page is the one I usually revise the most, struggling to suggest the setting, main characters, and theme. A good first page of a novel has a voice that might capture the attention of busy people. It provides details that convince readers the speaker knows this world, while building mystery and hints that something will go wrong.

I'll come back to these standards, but each day begins with where I am more than what I hope to accomplish. How do I get started? Typing lots of wrong words until the right words come along.

Forcing Flowers

Inspiration may be found in a hoe or a shovel as often as in a flowerbed. I'm a practical, gritty New Englander who doesn't expect blood on the page, but I'm not against signs of sweat. I believe, first of all, that everyone has something to say, and, second, that it may take a long time of being lost in a paper wilderness before we find a good and true story. The best we can do is keep typing, while staying ready to catch what often comes in disguise and without invitation.

Lately my nights have been broken by crying from our old dog who can no longer manage the stairs to come huff near my head to let me know it's almost time for breakfast. I plod downstairs. After I give our Labrador Retriever a few pats, she plunks down her head and goes back to sleep. I curl up on the sofa to keep her company. I have misgivings about this routine, but a bit of good that's come from it is when I'm lying between wakefulness and sleep, instead of focusing on poor-tired-me thoughts or whether we should invest in a sofa bed, I turn my thoughts to my work in progress. This sleepy state sometimes gives birth to a few lines. But would they have come if I hadn't been writing the day before?

Those waiting words remind me of the barely-budding forsythia branches I recently broke off, stuck in a pitcher of water, and left in the pantry. Every day or two, if I remembered, I added a splash of lukewarm water. Once they opened into yellow blooms, I put them in the kitchen, where they were admired by a friend who's a professional gardener. She asked about my technique for what is called forcing, a strange term for what basically means bringing branches to a warmer place and offering water. My friend told me that she'd tried different rooms, experimented with different amounts of light and various water temperatures, but never succeeded in getting her forsythia to flower. Did she try too hard?

Writing isn't exactly like forcing flowers, but too much

effort might get in the way. Sometimes I make myself sit before my computer, telling myself to toughen up. But I prefer to think of time sitting, as still as broken branches, as a gift to myself. Anything can happen as I draw from what I know and what I don't know. What once seemed complex may look simple. What seemed simple turns layered. Ideas may fall as quietly as feathers or clatter like a teacup on a saucer. There's no dropping to my knees or chanting and rarely the lighting of candles, because I'm kind of shy about what seems a little bit holy. I just give a quiet nod to show my respect for imagination and other mysteries.

Slowly, silence starts to feel less like a foe. Words quietly nod back.

Uninvited Guests

I like to write first drafts on yellow pads while perched on the window seat. When I'm ready for some distance from those first words, to see them fresh, I transcribe and change them on my computer, sitting at my desk or, for the third time this year, on the porch. Past the screens, tiny lilac leaves have sprouted. Hyacinths and daffodils have poked through the ground. A glass of iced tea and a stack of poetry books sit by my elbow. Sometimes the small white dog yaps at airplanes. The big middle dog alerts me to trucks or wild turkeys in the yard. The old Lab doesn't move much, but thumps her tail when I pass by to get more ice and lemon.

I'm working, though this doesn't look like an office, with a table covered with flower-printed cloth, no phone, just the hum of bees and an occasional shuffle of paper. I hear part of me sending another part to work and a voice plotting small rebellions. One me doles out advice, while the other runs off to check email *(What if I got a note from an editor? What if she can't wait five minutes for a response?)*. When the porch starts looking crowded, I give names and wardrobes to the different people in my mind. This helps me decide who I'll ask to linger and who I'll soon show to the door.

The rebel writer is told she's the only one who can write the book tucked in my files. She shrugs. She's reminded that the beginning is always the hardest part and of how happy she'll be when it's done. Another shrug. The disciplined writer stops lecturing and turns to bribes and tricks. She tells the one who's wondering if it's too early in the day for cookies that it's okay to shirk the task at hand, but she should tackle a different page. Or that the morning will be devoted to tidying, finding places for stray sentences. Switching from one scene to another can look like procrastination, but when I feel stymied with one, moving to another makes me return more eagerly to the place I left. Sometimes new ideas even roll in. What started as cleanup can lead to engagement, and it doesn't matter that the work is happening in Chapter Three instead of where I began.

Don't I need to get the car inspected?

It's not even the last day of the month.

We need milk and lettuce.

Aren't there always empty spots in the fridge?

A new project seems more stops than starts, whether or not that's mathematically possible. While I shuttle between excitement and fear about a new path, the rebel writer wonders whether it's too early or late in the season to transplant the iris. She craves too much salt or sugar. Some scenes are still warm on the page when I recognize they don't have the spark that tells me, *This is sound.* I need stillness to hear my own mind, though good ideas have surfaced while I've been dashing from here to there. But that's not a technique to count on, and it works better when I've spent the morning at the computer.

We can forget how much writing can get done if we just stay in our chairs. The daily habit, more than the number of hours or minutes put in each day, is crucial to the balance of being demanding and kind to our needy and distracted selves. I'm showing up for my imagination every day, so that sweet but fickle part of me won't wander too far. I want to be ready for the first sense of something aha-like, which isn't the sound of a muse plopping beside me, but astonishment at what I didn't seek, like an unexpected letter or a bird that skims by when my head is down. I'm grateful for each old and new idea, some upscale, some looking like they came from a bargain bin. I'm not fussy, but glad even for gifts I wrapped myself.

Falling in Love with an Unwritten Book

Falling in love means swooning, but also hesitating and falling. I feel giddy one moment, and the next declare my work a disaster. Writing a new book creates a place crowded with second and third thoughts. Some mornings I revel in the brand new shine of each detail. But by noon, I find it just plain hard to pay attention to the vast unknown, where new ideas crawl or leap from corners. I wish I had guides who could tell me if a single idea is good. Wondering if I should do this, that, or their opposites, I crave certainties, but no one can tell me, "You got that right," or even, "No, that's not it yet." I set down raggedy-edged scenes or bits of dialogue in the haphazard ways they come, trying not to mind whether they'll stay for the long haul.

Intimacy bumps into loneliness as I find layers within stories. Before I'm certain whether this is flirtation or true love, it's too soon to show even a chapter to my husband or my critique group. I have to work things out myself through the getting-to-know-you stage. It's usually best to even avoid confessions over drinks. While friends may listen to tales of flesh-and-blood romance, most aren't curious about a new relationship with pages. Besides, like many writers, I'm superstitious, perhaps another word for anxious, and don't like to reveal details that may turn on me tomorrow.

Some people yearn to spend all their time with a new love, but it seems that keeping constant company with a fresh-off-the-fingertips manuscript makes the rest of the world seem so very attractive. I wish the phone would ring, consider organizing my files, and wonder if it's time to check on the status of old manuscripts. Sometimes the last isn't entirely procrastination. Most of us aren't starting from a vacuum. Other manuscripts and books came before. Counselors advise taking plenty of time between an old and new relationship, but I like to start a new book when the last isn't entirely finished, winking at chapters that will be there to greet me instead of blank paper when one book is done. This overlapping means I have to be careful that as one manuscript makes its way into the world, my pleasure, regret, or fear doesn't color my feelings about the new.

I'm back to wondering if what I have can be worth a year or two or three of work, or whether I should start something else. Wait. These doubts are familiar. This is writing, something I know from every day, and not just the part we call starting out. Maybe this is a book after all.

Trillium

While heading to my writing room, I remind myself I've chosen solitude. I've been taking such steps for years, but it can still feel like a long way up the stairs. Today there's no bounce in my knee. I sit down and produce clumps of broken sentences and margins riddled with directions: *Fix this! Straighten out that! Check this fact.* I've got a main character, a theme of sorts, and a rickety plot.

I start out slogging, then lo and behold, by the end of the morning a once-dusty image starts to gleam. Once I start messing around with half sentences and finish a few, a familiar contentment, or at least tolerance of sitting, returns.

By mid-afternoon I'm ready to leave my desk. The breaks in my writing day used to coincide with picking up my daughter from school. Now Emily is beautifully grown, but the rhythm sticks with the dogs, who circle the computer at three o'clock to remind me it's time to head outside.

Stepping away can have its writerly rewards, as long as I make sure I have something to step away from. On lucky days, the writing continues in my head. Old sentences jiggle into new places. A bit of conversation continues. A motive springs up. A little time off can give me a distance that helps me see flaws, which I can then approach from a new angle.

Even less lucky days are good. The dogs find interesting things to smell. I get to stretch under sun or rain. While walking along a trail yesterday, I spotted white trillium growing by a bog. Wanting a closer look, I stepped carefully around the flowers, but didn't mind the muck. My feet got soaked, which didn't lessen my enchantment. I felt like a child finding a secret forest, feeling both alone and in splendid if invisible company. Here was a place of secrets, and at the moment every one of them benign.

Growing a Book

Early ideas may be as small as seeds, which gardeners can scatter, while writers seem bound to dive after them into the ground. It's not particularly pleasant under the earth, though with the right clothing, one can get along. Ideas grow in the dark, and that's where I've been, roughing up the soil, pushing around seeds to nestle or get lost. Gardeners don't expect everything they plant to grow.

These days I just tend perennials, but back when I had a vegetable garden, I never liked thinning out carrots. This meant I got a lot of scrawny and twisted vegetables. There's just not room for every one. It's better to be brutal. Here at my desk, I'm still coming up with bad ideas and even okay ones that I'll pull out later to make room for the best. So I wait and watch sprouts push through dirt. After some vigorous weeding, it's starting to look like a garden. I mean a book.

I choose a title that I might change tomorrow. Between pages, I switch point of view, and not in an avant-garde way. Images flash and burn out. Characters come and go or evolve, trying out and losing traits. But I'm becoming attached to some, and after tossing around handfuls of ideas that didn't sprout, there's a sentence I scribbled *ta-da* beside and haven't yet deleted. There's still enough murk in these drafts that anything could happen, and I try to let that be good news.

In the manuscript garden business, we have to not only conjure the seeds, but the earth, water, and sunlight, so there's bound to be lots of words, and we're bound to pull many out. We want to be as contented to be the person wearing overalls and driving a truck full of compost as the one who cuts a sweet bouquet or rakes a rough plot where a story can grow. We let things grow, then snip, over and over, practicing the gardener's faith. The soil doesn't look like much. But flowers and fruit have grown from patches of dirt before, and they will bloom again under the great sky.

Finding a Way toward Home

Back when my daughter was a teenager, we were leaving Boston when I took a wrong turn out of an enormous parking garage. The street we were looking for wasn't there, and I had to make a swift right or left. Either direction was wrong, but I couldn't stop or back up. Beside me, Emily was freaking out as I headed down a dark street in a city famous for fast drivers and bad signage. "We'll never get home," she shrieked.

"We will." I felt like screaming, too, but kept my voice calm. "There will be signs for the Mass. Pike somewhere, and we'll get out of here."

"We don't know where we are! We're stuck."

"Nothing looks familiar yet, but it will." I wanted to slam on the brakes, grab Emily, get out, and run. But with cars and trucks speeding ahead and behind, I couldn't brake in the middle of the road. And eventually – I'm here to write this tale – we spotted a sign and found our way to the home of the seemingly calm driver who was shrieking "Eeeekkk!" inside.

Beginning new work, I often hear that inner scream. *What am I doing? Where can these images go?* I throw them down, let them cluster and scramble in new directions. If anyone looked over my shoulder they'd wonder how I dared call myself a writer. All I claim now is moving hands, which means work comes out that may get better from sheer force and volume. Or it may not. I visualize, with fuzzy edges, much of what I want to say, then stalk verbs and nouns. At some point I've got to choose quality over quantity. That revision comes later, perhaps tackled by the calm-seeming driver. I start with a traffic jam of language, and as if surrounded by fast cars, I keep going. I don't know how, but somehow I'll find a way.

What We Can and Can't Fix

About a week after I bought the sofa bed, expecting to spend at least a few months of early mornings there, I called my daughter to tell her there was one less dog in the house. We still have two, and I often meet my friend, Mary, at eight a.m. to walk her dog and mine and get our heads in place. Recently she complained about the unfinished carpentry work around her house. This theme has come up before. And, although I know it, she likes to point out she's married to a builder. That day he'd volunteered to help patch the roof of a friend of a friend. His kindness grated on her, though she admitted it shouldn't. But their porch steps sagged, or was it a problem with the railings? I listened, I did! Even if I can't remember the exact details.

Mary pointed out how she's visually oriented and that unfinished projects and tools under the coffee table disturb her. "I know," I said. I'm not fond of the piles of books and magazines that tower on our kitchen table. I like an empty-ish place to set my gaze upon, a refuge from my busy mind. I can manage my usual worries about my daughter who lives across the country and editors who don't answer my emails, but lately the noise in my head is louder with concern for my friend, Pat, who I met almost thirty years ago in a Connecticut high school where I taught English and she taught Special Ed. We often ate lunch in her room where students who couldn't remember locker combinations or found the corridors brutal came to collect books or jackets they stashed there. Pat and I used to talk about the students we had in common, disturbing decisions made by the principal, our newish marriages, our dreams of having children, and the contents of our salads.

After I stopped teaching and moved back to Massachusetts, finding out that our husbands enjoyed each other's company tightened our friendship, as did the birth of my child. Pat and Ed became like an aunt and uncle to Emily, joining us for holidays, dance recitals, and family birthday dinners. After a recent gathering, Pat called with news she hadn't wanted to tell me then and spoil the celebration. Her colonoscopy showed cancer that had spread. A lot.

Mary and I kept walking. She said, "I realized how bad things were when I started fantasizing about moving, though I really love my life and where I live."

Yeah, we can't just move from our houses, bodies, or worried minds. Then how do we get to a peaceful place? I know the piles on our table will get bigger before they get smaller. I can talk with Pat on the phone most days, but I can't cure her. My daughter in California will decide her own future, have successes and setbacks, and that's just what should happen at her age. All I can do, really, is try to "let it be," as Paul McCartney sang in one of his loveliest of many lovely incarnations.

I still want piles un-piled now and then. Porch steps or railings should get fixed. Cancer should get cured. But if what we want to happen doesn't, life, with all its clutter and uncalm, will go on. At my computer, I've got to step in sometimes, but also just let my characters breathe, speak, and act in ways that are perfect for today's imperfect draft. New ideas may ask for only a little quiet time. Fortune-tellers need china and tea leaves to glimpse what can be, but also an open space over an empty teacup that invites simple gazing.

Second Chapters

Writing a first chapter is like tracking down the perfect outfit for a big occasion, then knowing the hem needs to be adjusted, or the right scarf found, while already having second or seventeenth thoughts. Did the scarf change the color scheme? Do the shoes clash? Should I start over? Writers could save ourselves a lot of fuss and time if we could just start with the roomier, more forgiving, second chapter. We're older, and the outfit doesn't seem quite as important, and if it's a little bit wrinkled, so what? We've set up the characters and can let them speak. A second chapter doesn't have all the bother of pulling in readers with neither too much nor too little information. Instead, it's time to develop what's at stake in the small world we created. We've brought readers through, but can we keep them? Maybe we should haul out the ironing board one more time.

Like every chapter, my second one will go through lots of drafts. I spend mornings dreaming up sisters, brothers, and friends for my main character, then kill off some by the afternoon. But because the second chapter isn't as delicate or slippery as the first, I keep coming back to chapter two when I stall on my way forward, peering for threads I might be able to use. Looking back over my own work is a little like reading as a diligent English major. Themes or symbolism can slide into view. As a college student, I never wanted to take symbol quests too far, and I don't want to take them too far as a writer, either. The trick is to keep a spirit of play, like someone carrying a plastic toy shovel for digging, but not a sharp-edged spade. We should forget the vocabulary of someone who's infatuated with literary theory. Instead, register differences such as those that might come from describing someone's hair as silver, tin-colored, or some other variation on metallic. We need to make a choice and move on without leaving the fingerprints of an author who thinks too much. Sometimes a rose is a rose, a bird is a bird, spring is a season, and swings, seesaws, and slides are just part of a playground.

I keep going onward, but looking back, sometimes even tossing ropes ahead at what might be a corner of the book's ending. Backward glances may reveal something I'd overlooked before, the way new feelings can rise from old photographs, or memories of someone's long ago words, pauses, or gestures may suggest something I missed at the time. Most of us grew up with shadow stories that make us think, perhaps ten or twenty years later: *Now I get it.*

I hope such understanding doesn't take a decade as I return to a single scene in my second chapter. The action there takes less than a minute and it's not particularly spectacular. There are no tornadoes lifting houses, boys flying through bedroom windows, or governesses sliding up banister rails. But it's a scene I found early on and feels important to me. As I shine it up I learn more, and look for other ways to suggest the theme. Maybe I'll even be so bold as to spell it out in a conversation. In *Save the Cat,* Blake Snyder tells us that in the movies, a minor character often states the theme within the first five minutes. Composers of musicals speak of early on songs that express the main character's yearning. In poems, too, I've often been swept in by images, and then found direct statements in the following stanzas.

So I'm looking for ways to slip a sense of what my book is about into the dialogue without being heavy handed. Or maybe I'll let my hands be just a little heavy, though I won't prop up placards with arrows. A theme should be like bubbles under the waves. We don't necessarily need a girl to tap her shoes and murmur, "There's no place like home," to get a sense of a journey's meaning. But sometimes lyrics or a wise person speaking up can help as we use language to hint, confound, speculate, draw arcs that cross between the past and present, tease forth what couldn't be seen at first glance.

Rain

———

Some writers grow up in families of storytellers, but my parents tended toward silence and short sentences. My mom was often in the hospital, and teachers or neighbors would ask me how she was. Echoing my dad, I'd say, "She's getting better." I became a writer partly because I knew there was a lot more to that statement, including how scared and sad I was, though certainly not every minute. Good memories include staying in some days at recess in second grade to write and draw small books. Two friends and I cut, folded, and stapled arithmetic paper, grateful that Mrs. Dunwoody seemed to understand not everyone wanted to jump rope, play dodge ball, or gossip in line for the slide five days a week.

During the next few years, I learned to scrutinize faces and surmise stories that others kept hidden the way our family did. I filled notebooks with the first acts of plays, half-finished poems, and first pages of novels. I liked writing small books with my friends and transforming my imagination into cursive, but when asked a question, my mouth didn't work properly. In seventh grade, my math teacher used to scold me and a friend for our soft voices, saying, "Speak up! How will you ever be cheerleaders?"

I looked for other ways to get my voice heard, though I had a lot of listening to do first, and didn't really lose my shyness until after college when I stood in front of a class of ninth graders, wondering whatever made me think it was a good idea to become a teacher. Quickly followed by: *You'd better say something, or they will destroy you.* And so I talked, and listened, and before too long sometimes even laughed.

I taught high school for just a few years, leaving to focus on writing and raising my daughter. When Emily was sixteen, I started teaching children's literature at UMass-Amherst, where I'd been an undergrad. My office with its plastic chair and steel table is nothing to rave about, but I love the view of grand trees, a pond that's home to ducks, an old stone chapel, and students walking or riding bikes. And being an alum, I have memories of talking about fiction in the room next door – my stomach doing flip flops when others read the stories I'd had photocopied.

I no longer wear cotton skirts, embroidered blouses, and dangly earrings from India, but, in honor of professors before me, an occasional tweed jacket and loud shoes. Some things don't change. The English Department building is pretty much the same, with perpetually scuffed cement floors and windows that time has sealed shut. And my stomach still flutters the first time my written words become public, which a long time ago was eleven other students and one professor around a rectangular table.

I remember a rainy day when this professor snapped open his black umbrella as we left the building and said he thought I had what it took to be a writer. Then added, "But it's a miserable life."

Over many years, on hard days I've thought of this blessing, which like many includes a curse. I've found my own way to write and to live with its uncertainties. I feel privileged to get a chance to use words to show what I know, to have an office in the building where I once stepped into the rain beside that professor, and to encourage some students. After I assign projects, some stop by to tell me their ideas for stories. I send them out fairly quickly, telling them to come back with something on paper, even if it's not great. Even if it's terrible. It's hard to see where an idea might go while it's still in the air. It needs a moving hand on pen or keyboard, which has the power to guide us to a new trail.

I learned my pedagogy not just at this university, but starting with Mrs. Dunwoody, who was a stickler for staying in place in reading groups, but who could teach writing just by being generous with arithmetic paper, handing three girls a stapler, and saying, "Watch your fingers." She trusted us to be our own critics. Now I encourage writers to remember a time when we wrote before thinking about an audience beyond those of perhaps two friends and our own hearts. To find strength in the sanctuaries, hideouts, gardens, or attics remembered from childhood.

One day I answered a knock from an undergraduate who'd handed me forty pages of an excellent beginning of a novel. We talked about the characters and setting, then I said, "Keep going. You have what it takes."

I didn't add that it could be a terrible life. She knows that it rains sometimes. And that every umbrella isn't black: some of us carry ones printed with cherry blossoms.

Creating Characters in the Dark

Walking the dogs with Mary while I talked about what's happening at my porch table, she laughed and said, "You make writing sound so complicated." There wasn't admiration in her voice. I don't mean to suggest that people in other fields don't work harder, or that I trip through mazes on my way to my computer every day, or that it isn't lovely to burst through bristling loneliness to find sweet solitude. But it can take a long time to find a daily focus.

Creating a character from a mix of whim and obsession can make me feel as if I'm floundering in deep water. I remind myself that a long distance swimmer might have to swim far with no markers. But doesn't she usually have a boat beside her, someone ready to pull her aboard in case of jellyfish, frigid water, sharks, or getting lost?

I want a safety belt, or at least to know what's going on. But as a poet and fiction writer, I pretty much have to wait for strangers to speak. Will they talk, and will the conversation be worthwhile? I feel awash in doubt, but am trying to rename that to "a space where something new can happen." I need to find a balance of what I draw from life and sheer imagination, both recollecting and letting memories go. I've been here, or somewhere like it, before.

Some fictional characters have origins in real people, often strangers, or those I've read or dreamed about. Something about the way someone bends to pick up a stone at the beach or turns her neck to see who's behind her while in line for popcorn may become the seed of a story, and even carry the importance I feel when an owl appears under moonlight in a fairy tale, all omen-y. I may feel a softening in my belly or a pinch behind my knees, as if a ghost entered the room. I might call it chance or coincidence, and may feel gifted or bedeviled. Or simply relief. Here's a place to begin, even if the process leaves behind the moment that set off the sparks.

We don't need to analyze this too much. We probably don't need to analyze anything too much. A novelist may be best off honoring whatever or whoever whispers to us by writing down some words and seeing where they lead. In fact, maybe it's that imbalance of knowing and not knowing, an awareness of life's quiet connections and many missteps, that start a story. An overheard sentence or semi-familiar gesture stirs a memory, so someone steps out of the shadows, though perhaps not too far. It seems good to work within a sort of dusk for a while, where characters are comfortable enough to confide in ways they might not at a dinner table.

Following these chance encounters takes a willingness to end up in the mind's back alley. I ask myself a series of questions to develop characters, which I've posed to students, though I suspect it helps to have the questions spoken by an instructor with a chicken-shaped timer by her elbow. Surprising answers may come from the measured box of time that lets writers hurry past the inner-decider-of-what's-stupid, which most of us have been taught to cultivate more than the hey-whatever-happens part of us. I'm talking neuroscience here, referring to the same principle that suggests the benefit of writing too fast or steadily for the discriminating part of our brains to catch up.

I've trained myself to hasten on my own, asking about characters' favorite dreams and worst nightmares, the contents of their handbags, knapsacks, or top bureau drawers. What was the most damaging thing their mother ever said to them? What was the happiest day of their life? What color is their favorite shirt? Does it have pockets, and if so, what's inside? Such questions can be useful, especially when limited time means we're bound to use our first thoughts, which can be developed later. It's often not so much interrogation as hanging out with someone that deepens a friendship in life or on the page. Characters we so-call-create have some sort of free will, and if we respect it, we may be swept to places we'd never have thought to go if we'd relied just on our judgment.

"Keep your pen moving," I tell students, and tell myself. Sometimes we slam through sentences into something never seen before, perhaps a character that readers will feel that they've met before. Some readers may even recognize themselves. And isn't that a prize?

I remember back a few decades to when a girl sat by our professor in a college writing workshop. She was nicely dressed, had a pricey haircut, and never stumbled over words. I imagined her as coming from a together family and being in a supportive relationship that would slip right towards marriage and well-adjusted children. She didn't seem anything like me. But once I submitted for critique a story based on my messy life, and I remember her saying, "This character reminds me of myself." And the professor, who was much older than us and male, nodded, too.

Was it possible other people carried secret flaws and memories of disasters? Of course. Writing calls for courage to face old feelings and new fantasies. The mind doesn't necessarily draw clear distinctions between grief and hope, imagination and truth. Sometimes an element missing from our work is right in front of us, clear as a shadow, and perhaps also that inexact. And some of that pain or joy can go into the writing to deepen, elevate, or point a way through a story that's never just one person's story, but the reader's, the writer's, and those conjured onto the page.

Keeping on when we don't see much light at the end of a draft is not for the faint-hearted. When things are tough, I remind myself that once upon a time someone heard me. I try to stay with my own voice, while keeping an eye open the way I do when talking with others, to see if my words resonate or are at least understood. It's me to you, or you to me, and always word by word.

T is for Tangent

As a professor, I spend a certain amount of time standing in front of a room making sure discussions stay on track. I never picked up the habit of a colleague who warns of tangents by shaping his fingers into a *T*. But in class the other day, I let digressions fly. We got into books about vampires and werewolves, which aren't on the curriculum. Opinions billowed more lightly than usual around the room, though I noticed some students near the windows kept quiet and slightly rolled their eyes. I smiled at them. Some of what was said was silly. None of it was backed up. But we had a little fun.

When I let matters shift beyond the syllabus or the planned structure of my book, I may not only enjoy myself more, but trip over something fresh. Sometimes we need to mind the clock, but it's also good to duck into an invented forest and wander through green and gold light. Sometimes I've gotten lost, weary, and sore, wondering: *Can anyone follow me here? Will my notes make sense when I get back home?*

Sitting down to write, I'm not welcomed by characters who've been waiting patiently as dolls shoved in a closet, ready for someone to come back and make them chat. Instead, at my computer I hear the voices that have been in my head all along. There's that list of chores, the emails owed, and fragments of scenes from the book I want to write someday but not now. I hear calls about all the other things I should be doing instead of working on a novel. I wonder what's taking me so long, and by the way, why haven't I heard from that editor about my last submission?

Buddhists compare the mind to a monkey that swings from branches, catching whatever comes its way. We may wish for more order, but can't force it, and would we be any happier with sedated monkeys or primates given only a few rails to play on rather than twisting vines and enormous trees? Eventually, we'll need to sort and sweep a path of bananas, ants, or sunbeams clear enough so that others can follow without making wild leaps or darting every which way, but first we have to let our minds not only be like monkeys, but a forest, too. Just as we might offer an open space where a friend can speak her mind, we should give ourselves an unhurried silence. And just as when we assure our friend that she can say anything, but she chooses not to, our minds may also balk. Instead of bounty, we get gossip, grocery lists, grievances, thoughts of cleaning the gutters or garage, or what-I-wish-I'd-said or what-I-can't-believe-she-said. These may be what we must pass on our way to deeper meanings. If we stick around and keep moving our hands, we can get past all the little thoughts about dogs, supper, movies, and whether we should get up and find a sweater to ideas we can use.

It's good to let in all voices, because slamming the door can shut out everyone. I tell myself I'm open to anything, and the idea-generating part of my mind believes me. I keep a notepad by my elbow where the list of things to get done rests on paper more comfortably than in my mind. Some of those emails do get written. And those voices that tell me I'm way off topic, point out scenes that not only don't belong, but should never have been written? I often put the critical voices right on the page. *Who do you think you are to write this? You're going to have to throw out the entire morning's work.* This isn't pleasant to look at, but it's better than having nasty voices drift between my ears. Giving them a place on paper seems to dim their power. And when the spoil-sporty words come back, sometimes they echo like the old ding of a typewriter hitting the end of a line. A simple chime, to which I can say: *You're wrong.* And move along.

Ways to Listen to the World

It's not easy knowing our daughter lives more than three thousand miles away, but Peter and I are proud that Emily learned to navigate around Los Angeles, a place that could hardly be more different than our small town. Our road has only a few houses and an assortment of goats, horses, cows, chickens, dogs, and peacocks that outnumber the people.

When we visited her recently, Peter claimed shock that she hadn't visited the La Brea Tar Pits, pointing out that they were only a few blocks from her apartment. Not being such a fan of the prehistoric as her Dad, though she has fond memories of making her princess dolls ride on his plastic brontosauruses, Emily quietly suggested that we go while she was at work. So Peter and I walked through a park where young parents pushed strollers and children tumbled on the grass under sycamores and dogwoods. We looked through a chain link fence at a lake pit with a statue of a mastodon lifting its trunk and tusks. Turtles sunned on logs.

Peter and I went into the museum. While he lingered before placards about mammoths, saber tooth cats, and wolves, I read about a farmer digging holes to plant peach trees and pulling up his shovel covered with something that was sticky, smelly, and shiny black. Before long, the farm was sold and archeologists set up tents and dug up bones, hoping to learn about who lived here twenty or thirty thousand years ago. Like stratum of earth, history is layered. It pulses like breath, shifts with moods and attention, rather than moving forward like a series of numbers. Each discovery makes possible another glimpse into the past or future.

The records of excavation here made me think of what I'd been reading for the book I'm writing. Archeologists in parts of Iraq, which used to be called Mesopotamia, and before that, Sumer, dug in sand for evidence of life long ago. Some clay tablets survived both flooding and fires for about four thousand years, providing evidence of what may be the world's first writing. The area is often called the birthplace of civilization because of this and the founding of cities and empires. Some time ago, as I leafed through a book about ancient battles for land, my eyes stopped at the name of King Sargon's daughter. Enheduanna was the first person known to have left writing that wasn't just lists or laws, but literature. The single sentence about her was put within parenthesis. My outrage at that diminishing punctuation, and the glimpse of another woman erased from much of history, strengthened my resolve to write about a princess whose father sent her down the Tiber River. Because Enheduanna was considered a sort of gift to keep peace between north and south, she was unlikely to see her family or homeland again. How would she make herself heard?

Peter and I walked down a La Brea path bordered by sage and looked into bubbling pits where tar is still being excavated. In the distance, I saw a little girl with many braids and a well-pressed dress who'd spotted two orange dragonflies flitting over the tar. She kept calling, "Look!" Her parents and brothers didn't turn, but I did. Maybe her parents didn't care about flying insects. Maybe her brothers thought she talked too much. There might be all kinds of reasons that they didn't seem to listen. Voices fade in the wind every moment of every day. Dragonflies beat brilliant wings, and only a few light on tar, and leave a lasting imprint.

Peter and I continued walking, but later, wondering why that girl had made my breath catch and my eyes fill, I realized that she'd led me to the theme of the book I was writing. I'd researched details and framed a plot, but like the bones in dark pits, theme takes time to emerge. Enheduanna had lived long ago and far away, but under her story of traveling and triumph was a girl whose voice kept getting lost.

Playing Statues

My critique group started meeting about twenty-five years ago. That's a lot of reading, analyzing, gossiping, supporting, tallying rejections, and occasionally bringing on the champagne. I wish I could say I never took these three people for granted, but I'm afraid I do as much as everyone I love, waking up only when I hear stories about groups splintered by jealousies, lies, bitterness, bad manners, or indifference. Dina, Lisa, Bruce, and I don't agree on everything, but we're our first and sometimes almost only audience, and we know that is precious.

I have fond memories of our early years, bringing my then-baby to snooze in her car seat while we discussed things like whether we should cut five or fifty pages from a novel. We took turns meeting at each other's houses, so sometimes Dina's or Lisa's children would show up in their pajamas. When we met at Bruce's house, we three moms felt giddy to plunk into chairs without first sweeping off plastic trucks, dolls, or dinosaurs. There were coasters, and tables that warranted them.

As our kids got older and stayed up later, we called an end to our herbal tea and cookies and met in a coffee shop. When that shop began closing too early for us to linger, we switched from decaf cappuccino to glasses of wine at an Amherst inn. We catch up on each other's lives, then take out manuscripts we've read and marked. After all these years, we trust each other enough so that we keep our affirmations short, then lunge into the prickly, helpful words that follow "but." We pose questions about the characters, pacing, or scenes without evident direction. It's not our job to suggest ways to fix things, but send the work back to the writer, who may feel both energetic and overwhelmed with fresh possibilities.

But if the author invites us, we will come forward with suggestions of ways to change directions or step up the plot. Last night Bruce, Dina, and Lisa made me feel as spun around as I did as a girl playing Statues on a summer lawn.

Remember friends twirling you, letting go of your hand, and at some point yelling, "Freeze," when we'd stop with arms and legs like marble? My writer friends tossed questions onto the table: *What if he ... what if she ...?*

I felt dizzy from the barrage of possibilities, but when I sorted through my notes today, certain roads stood out as better choices. Sadly, they weren't the routes I'd been on. Less sadly, they were intriguing.

I'm not exactly starting all over. The time and place are the same, and some of the plot. But the insides of key characters have altered. Sometimes a shake-up can happen in my head, but brainstorming can also happen with friends, whose flurry of questions reminds me that I can make just about anything happen on the page.

Keeping a Journal

I start most mornings at the same kitchen window or on the porch, where I often ease into work by recording what I see. Not much changes. Maybe the color of my mug, the scent of my tea, the way the wind blows branches and, lately, the changing shades of green and sizes of leaves. I might watch chickadees and woodpeckers, while the dogs bark at squirrels marauding the bird feeder. On dramatic days, we see wild turkeys or handsome bunnies.

My journal may take five minutes or, rarely, several hours. The process changes because our minds and hearts change. We're not an assembly line. But while times can vary, some consistency to the habit is important. Just as a runner isn't wise to skip stretching hamstrings that were stretched yesterday, writers need to warm up every morning, waking up the connections between our eyes, hands, and words. Some people who generally write prose begin their days composing free verse. The subjects might not matter, but I aim to keep to what I can see, hear, touch, smell or taste, which helps to ensure that the language can stand on its own two feet.

As a researcher, I've read old diaries that have convinced me of the unlikelihood that a record of general feelings or grievances will render much meaning from a life. I usually wish people had written more about what they ate for breakfast or wore on their feet. But while no one may read what we write, a journal brimming with woes and their analysis can be useful if it clears the mind to let us return to something with more grit or polish. Putting complaints or concerns on the page sweeps them from my mind, so I'm better able to focus on the work at hand. It's not pretty, but it's a stage as necessary as a cake that doesn't look good before it gets in the oven or even while it's baking. Anyone who's sewn knows a dress or quilt starts from plain thread, scissors, and cloth. We can't judge the results from the process.

I save these journals along with drafts of books that haven't been published because they're not great, because parts of them haven't reached their potential, it's not their time, or for no particular reason. These piles of manuscripts are taller than my stack of eleven published books. I also keep folders from each book where I stockpiled distracting subplots, stray character descriptions, scraps of dialog, edges of scenes, and mangled metaphors. These folders are like an attic filled with outmoded furniture in good repair, some stuff that could be fiddled with and saved, and other things bound to get tossed. This hoarding eases the sting of cutting perfectly good sentences. A few characters and scenes have met each other in new books, though most have been passed along without ever making it to a published page.

When I recently cleaned some drawers and closets, I wondered if it was time to toss the old notebooks and folders. I don't expect to ever reread them, so why hold on, when there's plenty else I've recycled or trashed? Mostly I believe the old journals are junk, but at least for now I'll keep them, along with stones I've gathered that matter only to me. But matter. Maybe not for what they are, but for what they let me see and briefly hold. The old may make me see something entirely new.

The Daydreamer in History Class

I enjoyed folk and fairy tales as a child, but I sat through some retellings mostly to keep a place by my father's elbow. Once my older sister could read by herself, she moved on to British fantasies with made-up maps. My younger brother developed a taste for superheroes and science fiction. But by the time I could explore a library by myself, I chose books about ordinary girls who lived among animals who didn't talk and between walls made of wood, not gingerbread. Carpets stayed on floors. Cupboards weren't portals to other worlds. My family's old Grimm collection became a prop when I pretended to tidy up a small house in the big woods.

In school, I took history classes that covered centuries or countries within paragraphs, stressed conquests, and left out most women, but I found a place for myself outside the classrooms, cherishing orange-covered books about the childhoods of girls like Helen Keller and Betsy Ross. I read *Little House on the Prairie,* then *Little Women,* then *Gone with the Wind.* I remember parts of those novels with affection, while I was glad to leave other aspects behind as I started writing my own books set in the past. Then, working within a small space to say a lot, my thoughts turned back to the economy of fairy tales. Once upon a time, descriptions of real bowls of porridge and a row of three rumpled beds had made me believe in talking bears. It seemed likely enough that bean plants, which I'd seen, could lead to a pot of gold, which I had not. Cinderella's story could be a plain old entreaty to dream if it weren't for the glass slippers I could imagine click-clacking and a coach that smelled like pumpkin pie.

We may read history as we read fairy tales, looking for ways that hope or fear can turn to courage. But as I chronicle lives set back in time, I try to avoid abstract words, which are apt to wiggle into unintended meanings or almost no meaning at all. Summary makes most of us sleepy. Just as magic mirrors, spindles, strands of wool, and strewn breadcrumbs help us cross into realms of wonder, I've found that some objects treasured by people in the past help me to slip back in time. Imagining what it would be like to keep my grip on a vine while peering past clouds, trembling at the voice of a giant, isn't so different from wondering what it would be like to become a world-changing poet, artist, or scientist. And writing historical fiction or poetry, leaning into history, then stepping back, isn't so different from playing dress-up, the way I did as a child with my grandmothers' old skirts, petticoats, shawls, and shoes, pretending that I lived on the frontier, asking myself: *What's wrong with the well? Why has the cow lost her appetite? What's that terrible noise in the distance?* These questions stirred plots that moved into theme. *Who are we? Where can we feel at home?*

Researching is like looking for the right hat to lead to the particular people and places that both limit and inspire me. When it's time to shift from facts to fiction, I shake off my library-probing jacket and let people chatter and act out. The feelings that bring a character to life might be right in front of me. I may borrow the blue of someone's shirt, the texture of elephant-ear-shaped leaves outside a cafe, the rattle of the wind through a gate, or an overheard phrase. Sometimes these just add color or change the rhythm. Often, what I put in gets cut. But some small images or bits of voices refuse to leave through each round of trimming. I hunker over these details, ask "Why are you here?" and really try to listen. I hang around, which we may call revising.

Why does a face or an edge of a dream haunt us? Maybe we should stick with it until we get at least of a hint of an answer. In his essay *Three Ways of Writing for Children*, C.S. Lewis wrote about how he thought through pictures, comparing writing to bird watching. He remembered a flowering currant bush and a toy garden his brother brought into the nursery, and the sense of longing – "though not for a biscuit tin filled with moss" – that stayed with him through his life. He also remembered a wardrobe that he and his brother played in when they were small. When C.S. Lewis was sixteen, he had a dream of a faun under a gas lamp in a snowy wood. More than ten years later, he began a story called *The Lion,* then put it aside. During World War II, children lived in his big house to escape bombing in London. All these images remained within him until he was fifty, when he put them into the books with a wardrobe that's a delightfully specific portal, crammed with soft fur coats, but that may let trespassers through to another world.

Some of what makes us grieve or celebrate may go into our writing to deepen, elevate, or point a way through writing that's never just one person's story, but the reader's, the writer's, and those imagined on the page. Writing is a bit like dropping breadcrumbs, making a path that shows a way out of all the forests we enter. One true story is that if an orphan, a princess, a boy named Hansel, a girl named Gretel, or anyone at all can find a way out, so can we.

Jeannine Atkins

Three Sisters at the Table

Writers sometimes look as if we're people who can't be pushed around. We set up and stand by sentences that look as inevitable as the shape of a life does when looking back, but we're as familiar with dithering and ducking as we are with conviction. We forge ahead trying to keep faith that our plot will hold up, while simultaneously wondering if everything will fall into a theme that anyone will care about. Writing is a tussle to get all the selves within us to get along.

When flipping open my laptop, three less-than-solid guests appear at the porch table. I invite in Confidence, but also set out lemon scones for her difficult sisters, messy-haired Uncertainty and the narrow-eyed Critic. Confidence wears a soft sweater, sparkly earrings, and once in while the pointy glasses I wore in fourth grade, though no one expects me to fill notebooks as quickly as I did then. Uncertainty favors filmy dresses and the wrong kind of shoes for work. She daydreams and offers peculiar but necessary gifts, which the Critic may wreck or at least hold to the light to check for cracks or stains. The Critic wears pricy suits and heels she likes to hear click. Her hair is swept back from her unblemished forehead, but her fingernails are chewed. She jabs her finger, pointing out everything I failed to do, all signs of the unlikelihood of anyone ever reading what I've written. She tears into drafts before they've had a chance to breathe. She never quite learned that I can't settle on the right sounds or meaning on the first try, and shuffles through discarded paragraphs, kicks pages studded with questions that mark my way. She can't tolerate the mess that must be made, so I tell her to go sit in the corner. She'll get her turn.

Starting out or even in the middle of a manuscript is no time for measures of what's good or bad. But I don't boot out the lady who's tapping her too-high heels, because I'll need her intelligence at the end of a draft. And if I let her mutter in the corner, her opinions about not only worthless words but my audacity in calling myself a writer start to sound silly. Sometimes I type out her accusations, then not much later cover them with a wash of blue and hit delete. That's kind of fun.

Confidence makes brief visits at the heady but fraught beginning and now and then along the way. While I stick to milky tea, she slugs back tongue-burning black coffee. We both throw up our feet onto the table and laugh. For a while I write more words than I cross out. Then in strolls Uncertainty, the middle sister. I try to greet her with more warmth than I feel, for she reminds me that feeling my belly tighten is a sign to keep going, not to stop. She bats away questions like: Why can't I know what will happen? Why can't I get to the end faster? I remember that a mangled sentence or scene may lead to one I need.

Writing can ruffle us up. On paper, we want to connect more than instruct, and we may do that most when writing from places we don't necessarily show when we're trying to impress people with our poise. So I pour another cup of tea for Uncertainty and pass her the fresh strawberries. When Jane Austen was young, she filled notebooks with bold handwriting. Few words were crossed out, while her later notebooks show handwriting that seems more hesitant, with slashes through sentences. Writing means being aware of the spaces between what's just under our hands and a vision of ways we want words to eventually line up. Even as I make assertions, I keep aware that I can turn them around. I'll let a character do something, then pause to see if she has another idea. I want to be certain enough to make a mark with words, while remaining uncertain enough to question whether my vision is clear. We have to balance pride in what we put on paper with a willingness to tear it all away.

At some point we have to commit to characters and what they do, but first it's good to be open to changes, perhaps turning a girl into a boy, or, if we choose, a wolf, an ant, or a zombie. We can change a city into a town or forest, or switch a village for a metropolis. *What would happen then?* is a question to ask through the early drafts. We take one sure step, the next tentative, but within that hesitation we may find our best prizes. We first imagine, then impose.

Which brings me back to Confidence, who showed up at the start and sticks around more often as I end a piece, sometimes willing to stare down the Critic. Once in a while, Confidence even wiggles into a cheerleading outfit and lets loose with rhymes and pompons. The trick is to be careful who to listen to when. Just as when we, say, get a new haircut, we know who we can count on to be polite and who will be honest, then choose which one to ask, "So what do you think?" Sometimes we just want to feel good about ourselves. Other times we really want to know.

I'm getting closest to where I need to be when the whistles or sneers fade, and I'm just in the story. Then, at last, all three sisters sit at the same table. Soon enough we'll raise our glasses, and say, "I couldn't have done it without you."

Nests, Gardens, and Forest Paths

Some writers find the word "setting" dull, as if we set, and that's the end of it. It's not. Time and place aren't static, and setting provides not mere background, but glimmers that can lead us forward or any which way. The details of houses, landscapes, and private drawers, the places where someone rested her head or put her hands, can suggest a framework to work within. I like to begin by focusing on a place in a particular era, because while setting doesn't seem as full of possibilities as character or as glamorous as theme, which we can argue about all afternoon, it also seems less threatening. Setting reminds me to stick beside my characters and try to see what they see.

If a place stirs my curiosity and actions offer at least an edge of a plot, I read to find out more about what someone did and when and where she lived. I may not know why I'm drawn in, but write to understand the pull, finding buried connections that may not matter to readers, except, perhaps, from traces of feeling left by my search. I let rooms, towns, or woods that trouble or lure characters touch me, too, until I understand not so much what they mean, but where they fit in a story.

Setting can suggest emotion without resorting to telling and answer questions such as what does the main character love or hope to escape? To make sure that setting is more than the part readers skip in a book, I try to embed descriptions in small slices. Each should function as a place where characters feel different aspects of themselves or who they can be. A good photographer knows when to move in and when to step back. It's rarely wise to stop the action to take out the notebook and camera. Characters should interact, literally walk into something, or get a painful sunburn.

Writers can use a particular place to create a sense of order by deciding where to put a character when she heard some kind of call to adventure, found hope, or felt her belief in her family, who are usually central to her world, break. Characters might begin adventures from fairly ordinary places, such as the wardrobe Lucy finds in *The Lion, the Witch, and the Wardrobe,* which is stuffed with fur coats. We hear something crunch under her feet – mothballs? – then touch something soft, powdery and cold. Instead of furry coats brushing her face, Lucy feels prickly fir branches. The transformation of the particular lets us believe in the magic, just as the description of the barn that begins chapter three of *Charlotte's Web* acts as a portal leading to the animals talking for the first time. The development of the farm animals as seen by Fern to characters in their own right happens so seamlessly that we blink only when some people call this novel a fantasy. The old barn is a place of refuge as much as *The Secret Garden,* with its hidden bulbs, bluebells, sprawling briars, and a rotting swing, which let two angry children discover love.

Beloved places of the past are often a source of inspiration, as they were for C.S. Lewis, whose mother died when he was ten, bringing about a temporary loss of faith worsened by being sent to a boarding school that he remembered as being more horrifying than his stint as a soldier in World War I. His friend J. R.R. Tolkien moved from his home in South Africa when young, and spent much of his adult life creating alternative worlds. Even after P.L. Travers moved from Australia to England, she carried a memory of being ten years old and telling fairy tales to her younger sisters after their widowed mother announced that she was going to drown herself in a river, then left the house. The plan failed, but in some ways P.L. Travers remained obsessed with abandoned children and never stopped telling tales of homes that fit better than the ones her mother chose for her.

Whether we love them, leave them, or both, the places where we grew up shape us. I'll never forget the bedroom I had as a child, with its rumbling silver radiator covered with a sheet of asbestos and a doily; my miniature animals were set here. I remember the red linoleum kitchen floor that left blood-colored water in the bucket when it was washed. The way my brother sat at the dining room table cutting tiny slivers of butter and pressing them into a baked potato, so slowly, delicately, that the potato became too cold to melt the bits of butter, stretching out the dinner. This reminds me that setting is made up of time as well as place, for this scene might never have happened after microwaves became common.

Outside our house were trees we'd deemed best for climbing, views, scents, and shade. I came to know myself partly through fields surrounded by stonewalls and back roads where I bicycled. I'd learn more about myself as I discovered the history of Massachusetts, including how decisions were made about settling where certain foods could be grown and ideas find havens. I was raised on a religion that scholars speculate conceived God as great, vast, and invisible because Judaism and Christianity had their origins in deserts under big skies, while people in Greece and Rome, who lived by the warm blue sea, had happier, more humanlike gods and goddesses. Some theorize that in the mountains of Asia, it must have been natural to assume that ego disappeared amid the natural glory. Earth and vistas shape our faith.

How does a landscape make someone's life seem larger or smaller? As we wonder why a place claims us, we may find a way toward theme. What does the main character learn? What insight about life does she need to understand by the end that she doesn't know at the beginning? While we want to be able to say somewhere in our process what our book is about, and make sure each chapter if not each scene somehow addresses that, theme is not our job to state. The great *Why* can't be answered or even asked in a sentence. Instead, we can show where someone stands, where she wants to go, and what may get in her way. Look around. What's under someone's hands? What's outside the window?

Tugs that Carry Us Through

Even if we don't make claims about fairy dust or lightning bolts, the word *inspiration* may conjure something swift, flashy, and strong enough to knock us toward paper. My books have begun with some aha-moments, but ideas – small, vital, and unspectacular-looking as seeds -- seem minor within the scale of the work. Inspiration is necessary and lovely, but perhaps not as vital as habits that get me to my chair, carrying on whether or not I'm lucky enough to ever again feel the initial shock of recognition. What matters most is whether my intrigue turns into a sense of responsibility, a term I'm using not with its sense of chore, but more like that of a parent who may rue sleepless nights, but delights in a small child's goofy smile or fuzzy hair. The connection deepens as one question gets answered, while more come up. A scene or image seems to reflect another, toppling both into motion. That's when I know I have a book.

As I look for ways not to explain or describe but to embody feelings, stories may grow between my mind and words on the page. The writer-in-me seems to be connected to the girl-in-me who chose the orange-covered books about people from that past that brought me hope, stamina, and pleasure. Much of my work begins with people who did something that made my heart beat hard. I'm drawn in the way people fall in like love, first admiring, then both recognizing something in common while being stirred by what remains mysterious. Sadly, words like biography, poetry, and science don't make many editors' heart go pitter-pat. I want my work to be published, so I examine my themes with care. But I come back to understanding that it's my own heart that keeps me alive.

Is a promise of connection between author and subject necessary for a good book? Do readers need to find traces of the creator in books or art, sometimes put in deliberately, sometimes not, but perhaps as inevitable as the shapes of sentences or the habitual angle and pressure of a painter's brushstrokes? I don't know, but I think it's necessary for me. I surround myself with cherished books and people who give me yellow legal pads for my birthday, or send kind emails, or ask what I'm writing and don't inform me about its sales potential, but instead just look to see if my eyes are shining.

As I work on a good day (which still doesn't mean it's one without sighs and distractions), the tug between me and my newborn creation fades in and out, but what's lovely is when the tug eventually seems less from my side and more from words I set on my screen. Is this like a potter paying attention to the feel of clay under his hands, the force of a spin that his feet pumping the wheel has set in motion? Is it like a singer struggling to make her voice match the music she means it to be? Maybe some paintings aren't complete until just the right traces of the artist's hands blend with the subject. That sense of being with work that speaks to me as much as I speak to it may be the transformation William Butler Yeats imagined when he wrote, "How can we know the dancer from the dance?"

Feathers

Peter and I celebrated our anniversary with a weekend in Maine. While walking along the rocky coast, he asked if the ocean inspired me. Yes, in that peace and a wider frame of mind come from the shuttling and spray of waves, pebbles clattering as they're sucked back in. No, in that I won't go back to our room and pen odes to seagulls, horseshoe crabs, frothy waves, or a taste like French fries on my tongue.

I expect most poets who often take nature as a subject, such as Robert Frost and Edna St. Vincent Millay, don't see a wall being mended or irises shooting up and dash home to write about stones or flowers. Frost wrote *Stopping by Woods on a Snowy Evening* on a warm day when lilacs bloomed. Visiting Edna St. Vincent Millay's home-turned-museum, I was gladdened, in that me-too way, to see all the crossed out words in one draft of a sonnet. Scholars say she spent twenty years on some poems, which is a lot longer than an iris blooms.

Ideas rarely arrive in carefully sealed boxes, but turn up where we least expect them. Nature does offer inspiration, but much of it is through reminders of the peculiar and wonderful ways that beauty may greet us. My imagination is more apt to be stirred by small things than a grand landscape. Sometimes that's a broken seashell, catching the light. Or a smooth stone, small enough to fit in the pocket of the muse who was called Memory.

That afternoon, a bit of white down floated past the window at our inn, as a feather might have drifted about four thousand years ago. And in a serendipitous moment that wouldn't have happened if I hadn't been reading about a girl who lived in ancient Iraq, an old goose woman seemed to whisper in my ear.

Circling Through Verse

A friend I hadn't seen in a few months, though she's someone I've known since high school and lives nearby, recently asked me to take a walk. We met by a little post office in the town between ours, set off down the tree-lined street, then headed down dirt roads toward the river. Amid the green fields, past day lilies and Queen Anne's lace, we caught up on our lives. When we found ourselves back at the post office, Sue suggested we take another stroll, this time on the sidewalks. It was then that she told me about something difficult happening in her life. We made a loop past blocks of houses, and she suggested we keep walking. She told me still more on our third walkabout, while I nodded and tried not to make too many suggestions. On our last round I tried to really listen.

This has happened to many of us: someone asks to meet us, and we don't hear what's most on her mind until we're back by our parked cars. I make rounds like this through my writing, too, sometimes going deeper, other times looping into different forms and subjects. The book I'm writing now and calling *Conversations with the Moon* began long ago as a picture book manuscript about the origins of creative writing in ancient Iraq. An editor who'd published other books I wrote about women in history thought Enheduanna lived too far away and long ago for her life to gracefully fit within thirty-two bound pages. Besides, her name gets jumbled in a mouth.

She was mostly right. There's not much I can do about the name, except suggest splitting it in three if Enhe-du-anna works better. I couldn't shake my feeling that she should be better known, so I wrote a novel for readers about ten or twelve years old. This made a few eyes glimmer, but ultimately, they turned dull again. I put away the manuscript for a few years, then rewrote it as a novel for teens, focusing on the ways some may tackle loneliness by expressing their feelings in poems. I wrote a first chapter. My writing group said … something. They didn't gush, but they urged me to try again.

I revised off and on again during the years when I also worked on *Borrowed Names: Poems about Laura Ingalls Wilder, Madam C. J. Walker, Marie Curie and Their Daughters* and found an editor. After I finished my novel about Enheduanna, I sent it to her. A few months later, she emailed back that she liked it, but thought it would work still better as the sort of verse I'd done for *Borrowed Names*. Would I revise the prose to verse?

I noticed she didn't offer a contract. There was murmuring from me, and when I told the members of my writing group, raised eyebrows. Then one day, I went for a hike with a friend who writes both poetry and fiction. She quietly said, "I'd love for an editor to ask me to send her poetry."

I got it. I told myself I'd try revising about fifty pages and see what that looked like. I ripped apart sentences and chucked out paragraphs and pages, looking for images to salvage and shine. By the time I'd pulled apart thirty pages, I was pretty sure free verse was a better form. I committed myself to the project along with more rounds of research, which for women from the past, often means looking for clues among records about the men in their families. Much of what I learned about Enheduanna's life came from records of her father, King Sargon, and her four warrior brothers. Some fairly scholarly books cover her work as priestess and poet, but I wanted to show what came before the acts that brought her fame in her day. The quieter moments of history may be as important as what happens in a family between posed snapshots.

Though Enheduanna was a princess who lived thousands of years ago, she was not entirely different from any of us. We may not be sent across the known world to help unite an empire, but most of us have coped with sadness upon leaving people we love, and fear as we try to make new friends. I imagined a girl slipping off her sandals, picking up a stylus and clay tablet, contemplating the moon, and getting mad at her mother. How did she decide to impress cuneiform symbols into clay to depict feelings? We'll never know exactly, but poetry, a form that has long blended fact and imagination, gives me a license to work in the pulse between answers and questions. I looked for information, winnowing from the already spare historical record, like a person who spends a long time in an attic and returns with one small, revelatory object. I moved forward from the *what, where,* and *when* to try to answer *why.* Taking lots of words and leeway, I first fully imagined scenes, then pared them into poetry.

Will my girl get to eat a feast of roast lamb with thyme, fragrant grains, olives, figs, pears, and fresh hot bread? Hear gray pigeons croon? I don't yet know, and that's all right. Each new line suggests the next. I tone down some images, toss some others, and try out phrases in new places. I make slashes through stanzas and ask: Is this line crucial? This poem? I keep to the chronology, orderly as someone laying bricks. And when I get facts lined up, they seem to have the weight of brickwork. I remind myself then that the point isn't the walkway, but making a place to look at the sky. Bricks and mortar are necessary, but for a book that needs song as well as a story, there comes a time to put down the tools and kick aside broken bricks, slosh around the mortar, and let colors or textures remind me of one moment I can hold up to another. I don't want the story to take over and drag down the words, but I also don't want something so lyrical that they might drift away. I aim for just the right tension between what's revealed and what's held back.

Poetry ask us to slow down and savor sounds, whether they're rhymes at the ends of lines or within, the repeated vowels or consonants of alliteration. Each line should have a reason for being there. A clunky noise may be forgiven in a novel in which readers are gripped by characters, but a wrong note in a poem may stop the reader. I work line by line, reeling in vagueness, trying to put small gifts in every one. A word that glimmers, a shock in the rhythm, the smack of two clashing things coming together.

While I worked, reviews were coming in for *Borrowed Names,* including four with stars. "How many can you get?" Peter asked. I told him one from each magazine; these review journals aren't like *People,* which lines them up. Now Peter sometimes sweetly says things like, "Did you feed the dogs? And, oh, about those stars …"

It's nice not to have to be the one to bring them into

the conversation.

Thinking I might have found my best way to shape history, truth, and feeling, I revise like a madwoman grinding an eraser into rubbery dust. After a while, the stanzas look like stanzas. And probable poems turn into poems.

Fortunes

The porch is a little too chilly. The yellow irises are crunched, no longer stalwart, but limp from the rain. Hummingbirds have retreated, so the columbine look lonely. I fetch a shawl, fingerless gloves, and thick socks. My plan is to look straight out into the trees at the edge of the lawn and settle into the place where I left my characters. But I can't do this without taking note of my own inner twinges. I'm feeling a sense of spring with all its yellow and green loveliness, but also hints of loss as I think of Pat's cough, which may be from a cold, chemo, or cancer. We often talk on the phone, and she asks me to look up her symptoms, meds, or treatments on the computer, with instructions to edit grim news from my report. Internet diagnosis is dangerous, so my reports evolve into, "I think you should follow your good doctor's advice."

As I scan medical terms, my vision blurs as I remember things like the ordinary lunches we ate in her classroom, Pat reading picture books to Em long ago, and all of us riding waves on the coast of Maine. I try to recall which summer it was that sand got into the hummus in our pita bread, and when the tops of our feet got so sunburned, and which afternoon we collected a handful of blue and green sea glass. For most of the past twenty summers, Pat has stayed with us when we've rented a house in Maine. Will we all get there this year?

I manage some pages in my journal, but it's one of those days when it's hard to imagine how anyone anywhere ever wrote a book. Hope flickers when I'd rather it be steady. I took plenty of English classes that included tales of the tragic lives of writers. I don't believe that misery must be part of the profession, though none of us can entirely evade sorrow. Writers may or may not be more prone to depression than the rest of the population, but we do have to spend time alone, where all kinds of thoughts can swoop, and we'd best let them in, for pushing down fears or anger may send creative thoughts underground, too. My mom was the sort who advised, "Don't dwell on things. Leave the past behind," but I became someone who dwells for a living, sweeping rubble and dust from hidden stories.

Recently, I asked a friend about her daughter, who I remembered as writing enthusiastically as a child and teen. My friend's brow wrinkled. Her daughter is now an English major at college and seems to be not writing, focused instead on battling anxiety. We talked about how those may be connected. I said that, I, too, had loved writing as a child, but got stymied as an English major reading the greats. What did I have to add that William Shakespeare or Emily Dickinson hadn't already phrased better?

Learning to be a writer is partly learning how to cope with our own angst, aided by tips and murmurs from the clan. Things get easier when we accept that someone will always write with more mastery than we do, someone will write more clumsily, and many of us will write just fine, though our work may never be widely praised. When recovering from a rejection letter, I remind myself that on good days, writing helps me feel more balanced, instead of fraught. And as an author for young people, I may visit schools to talk about writing and crouch beside children whose mouths, often with missing teeth, crumple in concentration as they shape letters. Now that's a beautiful sight. I've talked in preschools where people about half my height have lined up at the end to hug me, and once, a little girl solemnly said that when she grew up she wanted a haircut like mine. This seemed less impressive as I took a closer look at her short, straight hair with bangs and realized my practical bob was pretty much like hers.

I'm lucky in my life, but like most people, I don't always bounce with a sense of my good fortune. I'm all for remembering rainbows after storms, but truth should be part of our conversations, too, and flowers don't bloom forever. In fact, there are days when we're too blue to water the geraniums, never mind pinch off the dried brown leaves. I know it's wise to be grateful for all the big and little things I have, to remember that having work rejected is better than being in a car crash, for instance. But sometimes I spill the half-full cups I'm counting. Wisdom is like a shirt that won't fit no matter how I turn it around or fiddle with the buttons, cheer as impossible to find as it can be to remember that a cold will end while we're surrounded by crumpled tissues.

Darkness, which reminds us of our vulnerability, guides us as much as light. I believe we have to go through rough places to see more clearly, but I also believe in being kind to ourselves. Each of us has to decide how much we can bear and when we need some cathartic complaining, another glass of iced tea, and perhaps another cookie, too. There's a time to hunker and wallow, but then get back to writing or at least watering the geraniums, which all these years I've never managed not to kill: there they are, with their helter-skelter branches and just when I need it, a burst of red or pink. Yes, I can fill a glass halfway.

The next day, I wake up again to the world where oranges are sweet, and eat oatmeal from a bowl my husband made. The dog wags his tail for no particular reason as he does every single morning, but now I stop to notice.

Letting Letters Set a Tone

Advice from a writing professor my freshman year in college has stuck with me through the decades. She took a look at my flowery language and suggested I take a break to write some letters home. My family was glad for some details, and I got the point that writing can be best when begun with a very particular audience in mind.

I've sometimes since taken a main character and written about her as if to an old friend. Or begun a section as a letter to her, asking the sort of sincere, casual questions we often reserve for people we know well. These questions might include: Do you have a favorite place to be alone? A favorite piece of clothing, animal, tree, or book? Did someone encourage you to do what you love? Did anyone try to stop you? What parts of your work are hardest? What mistakes did you make? What did you learn from them? Who or what do you love? What starts as a letter may turn into more of a conversation, and if my character seems chatty, it's best to let her speak, even, or especially when she veers off topic.

We don't always need to keep a particular audience in mind, but might remember that Beatrix Potter's letter to the son of her former governess turned into *Peter Rabbit*. *Alice's Adventures in Wonderland* might never have been written if Lewis Carroll hadn't rowed a real Alice and her sisters up the Isis River. *Winnie-the-Pooh* began as stories A.A. Milne told to his son, Christopher Robin, who was teased terribly in boarding school, and resented his father through his life. Maybe things would have been better if his father changed the name. But addressing just one person at a time, instead of the vast, vague public, can create the kind of tone and intimacy we trust.

Slim Books

Peter and I bicycled along a path that goes by several lakes, where we saw yellow water lilies and swamp marigold. As we pedaled, Peter, who's been scanning old photos from our pre-digital age, talked about how I wrote when we met about thirty years ago -- fiction on an electric typewriter -- and the way I write now. I often begin with window seat musing, jotting down words and phrases with a pen, then when starting the long work of revising, I reach for my laptop. The little noise of my keyboard is sweet company as I tap out free verse. As I get older and time feels shorter, I like to read and write slimmer books.

"Good writing isn't about just what is put on paper, but what's left out," I said. "Sometimes one line is all you need."

Pared lines seem a good way to approach history, which can otherwise feel overwhelming in its heft and scope. I try to unite the narrative impulse of *Let me tell you a story* with verse, both intimate and intense, and which sheds light on what's wrongly been forgotten. Robert Frost remarked that writing free verse is like playing tennis without a net. He wanted rhyme and meter to lend structure, which I get. But when people ask me why most of my verse doesn't rhyme at the end of lines, I say that poems set in the past give me structure enough. Imagery that's used one way in earlier poems echoes differently later. I draw lines between particular sights, sounds, and smells like the imaginary lines between stars that make up a constellation.

I balance being the biographer, who needs to be exhaustive, with the poet, who travels lightly. I wander through libraries for books about where Enheduanna lived and the company she kept, trying to answer both why my subject was forgotten and why she should be remembered. Researching feels like getting to know a friend, with affection deepening the more I learn about her. I'm often more taken with who quarreled with who or whose room was untidy than with the moments of great discovery or daring. I sort my finds into what's interesting, what gets in the way, and what order makes most sense.

We want people to read poems more than once, which means we have to make our way through them, I don't know, a hundred times? There's no need to count, but we need to backtrack and set things awhirl again. Once I get my facts straight, once I've described, say, a bird, with the slant of every feather distinct, I shut my eyes and listen for what flies, flutters, or falls. I shake the poems like doormats. Phrases tumble. Some are swept past the margins and stay there. A few find places in other poems. Some spots need a bit more mystery, and I nudge them around corners, away from the bright light, to let shadows do their work. Perhaps a slight or temporary break from realism or an offbeat angle will make me see something in a new way. An impossibly placed ear of a dog. An out of character remark. A sunset at the wrong time of day.

Looking for the right word is like approaching possible treasure with proper reverence. Then I trim some more, watching to make sure that not too much meaning disappears, leaving just enough to hint or provoke. I ask: What's too much and what's too little? How many birds can I get away with, and how can I make each wing distinct? How much alliteration, which I'm so fond of, is delightful, and how much is not? I take a stance like a hostess who welcomes in guests, but doesn't show them the whole house. My aim is to invite readers to make their own interpretations, leaving them guessing, but not deeply puzzled or lost. Line breaks or white spaces between stanzas can offer a way to enter silence that may tease out a place to hover or land with a soft thud.

"So what are you working on now?" Peter asked.

"My book about Enheduanna."

"Remind me who she was."

"Another obscure woman."

"But not for long," he said. "I can't wait to wear my Enheduanna T-shirt."

Research in the Afternoon

Back when Emily started school, I generally used those eight-to-three o'clock hours to focus on writing. Back then, the Internet wasn't a big part of my life, but research was. This meant going to the various libraries in our community and wiling away an hour or two before making choices that could fit in a big canvas bag. It was dusty work. The floors I ended up on between stacks weren't meant as seats.

After I took home my precious haul, those books cried out to be read, with one volume leading to another. Because fact finding is so compelling, and reading other peoples' words is generally easier than writing my own, I ended up making a rule for myself: I should write in the morning and could read old books only after three p.m.

There's no longer an eight-to-three routine in our house, but I still try to hold off on research to the hour that's wired into me as much as the dogs, who recognize their time to take a walk. My brain is as fresh as it will get in the morning, so it's best to write then. And reading after teatime, when my mind moves more slowly, works. I don't have to read on full alert as I don't want every recollection or recounting, just those that are bristly enough to bust through as I browse. And since I've spent the morning with my characters, I know what they might need. Some scenes change in my mind as I read, in which case, I take notes. I don't have a no-writing-after-three p.m. rule.

Once I started finding some information online, my research changed, but I still begin with books with raggedy cloth covers, rubber-stamped dates on pockets for cards, and less vetted lore. Like so much that's efficient, what we find online isn't necessarily rich or evocative. Computers offer us the highway, when sometimes we want back roads, detours with unexpected shops or peculiar gardens. But once I'm underway, I'm grateful for computers, which can swiftly answer questions about a date or what people might have eaten or been wearing at a certain time without consulting thick volumes. I can check about the color of cloth, but this might lead to a picture of a lovely scarf, and I want to know if it's available, and I think of a friend's upcoming birthday. Research can turn on a dime into distraction.

Much important research happens when we don't know exactly what we're looking for, but when we know what we need, we may find good material online. I recently wanted to know more about the birth of a calf. There is nothing like smelling hay, hearing vigorous breath while light slants into a stall. But if we can't get to a farm at the right hour, someone with a camera may provide a decent YouTube option. With a few taps of my fingers, I can not only find descriptions but videos of the intricacies of this or, say, how a potter shapes clay on a wheel.

How do we know when to shut off the computer and put away the tomes that we cull for readers, so that they can immerse themselves in another time and place? Could the last book from the last library give me just the detail I need? A favorite tale about the rewards of persistence comes from a scholar who was drawn into used book stores, heading to biographies of her subject though she'd read them all, then opening one and plucking out a folded carbon copy of a letter with the address of someone she'd been trying to find for many years. And he was still at that address. Can't you hear my contented sigh?

But there are darker stories. I know of a few excellent biographies that took twenty years of work. Other writers have spent even longer, perhaps waiting for still one more piece of information that can do justice to their subject. Finishing can be a biographer's curse. Just as we'll never find one lifetime long enough to do everything we want, we can't come to the end of a beloved subject without the little bit of force called a deadline, even if we set that time ourselves. We'll leave loose threads, but that's okay. We have scissors.

Slamming Through Walls

I now think of courage as a form of love, but I grew up associating bravery with lone heroic deeds, sacrifice, or being part of a swaggering team. None of this looked anything like me. Even when I played games like Robin Hood, I was aware that the sticks I used for arrows were more apt to flop to my feet than soar toward an imaginary foe. I couldn't see myself as Dorothy accidentally splashing a bucket of water on the wicked witch, never mind Gretel, deliberately pushing a murder-minded lady into an oven. No one wants to feel scared or vulnerable to being laughed at. One of the first signs of a child leaving childhood is when they're spotted flubbing up, and instead of moving on, they claim, "I meant to do that." Kids no taller than tables start wanting to look always in control, which may take many more years to learn is a mythical state.

I recently listened to two students give a presentation on fantasy writers, noting the paths characters take to other worlds. They showed a clip of the first *Harry Potter* movie, with our hero at the train station, blinking and gulping in front of what he hoped was Platform Nine and Three-quarters and an entrance to Hogwart's School.

"Don't stop and don't be scared," the mother of his new friend, Ron, advised. "Best do it at a bit of a run."

This is like the path to Narnia. In *The Lion, the Witch, and the Wardrobe*, the children don't know where they're going. Lucy slips through the snug coat-packed wardrobe to the big open forest, feeling both accepting of and astonished at everything she finds. In C.S. Lewis's *The Voyage of the Dawn Treader*, the children step through a painting, leaping without looking.

Can we do that? I'm not a child and I've been writing for a long time, so I'm well aware of words behind me and words I mean to write. Often I feel more obsessed with planning and cleaning up than shutting my eyes, spreading my arms, and jumping. News from the world past my desk can make me feel shallow-breathed, not in the mood for risks.

We all have real walls we have to face. But when it's time to write, can we let them fade into the color of empty paper? Be like the child who charges ahead without knowing where she's going?

Come on. Let's run straight at that wall. Or leap.

Summer: Moving Through the Middle

Midway through a book, much has been sketched out, but there's a long way to go. As we creep forward, tip backward, or shuffle sideways, we may feel forced to celebrate decisions that knock us back to the first page. While it's great to get congratulations when we finish a piece, the long stretch toward it is when we may most crave shoulder pats and cheers. The middle of a book lacks the sparkle of the beginning or the flash of an ending. One minute we brag about pages in the triple digits, and the next, we twist the plot, so scenes roll and unravel, with perhaps a few sentences salvaged. But there's no getting around the need to keep going, staying alert for surprises we can stumble on any day.

Where I Am

It's laptop-on-the-porch season, no socks or sweaters needed. I'm looking out at a pale blue sky. That might not mean much to some, but this summer in Massachusetts we haven't seen nearly enough blue. The breeze is neither hot nor chilly. And a murmur of bees comes from a flowering tree. When Peter left this morning, he said, "If you don't write at least a chapter today, something's wrong."

I guess that is a challenge. Perhaps halfway through a book, I don't have to wear blinders against the glare of the blank page. I'm past the battering questions of a beginning, when I might want to brainstorm with friends, but the work is not so polished that I'm looking for readers. The copy editor in me can keep quiet, instead of staying vigilant for puffy phrases and wandering sentences. It's a good place to be, but I'm smelling the husband-cut grass, wondering if I should clip the dried iris blossoms. Instead, I watch a bee circle the yellow day lily. I know there's life beyond what I can see. Where is the bear I saw two weeks ago? Will the phone ring? Will I answer? Never mind. There's not a lot on my calendar; I just have to remember that can be good.

Few of us actually sit for hours with hands tap-tap-tapping. Inspiration more commonly comes in bursts, often after lots of tea pouring, dog-letting-out and letting-in, refilling birdseed, penning grocery lists, and wondering if I could use some music or more distance from the cat. I put the tips of my thumbs and index fingers together, stretch my arms, and look through the diamond-shaped frame. Here is where I am: green grass, yellow and black bees, white blossoms. My not-great-but-could-be-worse back on the wicker chair. I cast a spell to be in this moment as I tap out on my laptop what's before me: an orange butterfly lights on the center of a flower, tastes pollen.

How Many Words? Who's Counting?

My walking buddy is away on vacation, but I'm still getting out with a dog or two. My big dog likes walking in the woods with me, but instead of sticking to the paths, Parker gallivants to check out swamps and squirrels. At almost nine years old, he's satisfied with a loop, or maybe two. And unlike Mary, I don't keep a pedometer (along with dog biscuits) in my pocket. I'm content to walk around once, but because I know that when Mary comes home she'll be listening to how heavily I breathe on the hill by our house, and because she'll ask, and because it's already embarrassing enough that this is my exercise, while she considers it just a prelude to the gym, I make myself hike two loops. But seldom the three we do together. With Mary by my side, I can make it past the bend because I don't want to be the laggard or interrupt the conversation. I can get around on the force of hearing the latest re her job, garden, opinions on health care reform, etc.

On the screened porch with my laptop, nobody's watching, counting, or cares much. I've got to make those laps and corners on my own. The middle of a manuscript offers new chances for minor triumphs and terrors. I haven't yet made every mistake or had to backtrack much or blow up bad chapters. But I flinch at sentences that were ripped in two before they were even finished. The structure keeps sliding around.

I know some writers, perhaps the same people who use pedometers, who are motivated by daily word counts. Whatever gets you sitting down is great. But tallying words is counter-productive when writing poetry, and even in rambling drafts of fiction, I'm not keen to measure words that are shoddy or perfectly good, but a bad fit, bound to be sent away the next day.

I'm tired of small steps forward and awkward ones back. But when I've written enough, a good phrase or turn in events startles me. Did the fresh idea come from the universe? My mind? The clutter I first created? Who knows? I take a moment to sit back and say something like: Oh wow. Sometimes I have to be grateful for even a few crummy words that break the blankness of the page. I remember that I wrote a good sentence once, and it can happen again. Maybe not in the kind of time I'd like, but then who's counting?

The Trellis in the Forest:
A Way Toward an Outline

All writers find their own ways to get from the first to last page. Some people outline first, though not all stick with it, but bend or wreck it along the way. John Irving says he needs to know the last sentence of his complicated novels first. Others agree with E. L. Doctorow that writing is "like driving a car at night. You never see further than your headlights, but you can make the whole trip that way." Writing can be as confounding as life, which dishes out surprises. I'm one of those who tend to create characters, give them a time and place, and let plot spring from their natures. Do I waste time with detours, or learn from byways and accidents that draw me deeper into new places? Maybe both.

Wishing I were the kind of writer who didn't have to backtrack, draw zig-zagging arrows, and stumble into a plot may be as futile as wishing to be a foot taller or shorter. I've been leery of outlines since my school days when I wrote them using Roman numerals and fancy indentations. Even more contemporary outlines made with lovely colored index cards and pencils still seem too much about pushpins and shifting things into a numerical order. I don't want something so neat that I'm afraid to swap pink cards for yellow ones or leave eraser crumbs.

Outlines work well for books that need a clear sense of how a beginning will sweep or twist toward an end, but I'm afraid if the plan is too plain and sturdy, the book can turn out flat as a billboard. I like to read with a sense that I'm missing something, that if I go back I'll find something new, as I could in a real forest. If the language is too purposeful, as it is in some outlines, I'm afraid it will lead to creating a forest as bland as one painted as a backdrop for a very amateur theater production.

But life is getting shorter and I'm reconsidering my stance on outlines. I can't pretend I know exactly where I'm going, so I'm working with a structure that leaves plenty of room to move. I carve it from material I've already set down, using the sort of language my novel will be made from. I imagine sowing a wild forest, complete with holes to stumble into, briars, and branches that might snag my shirt or poke my glasses, then building an enormous trellis to give it shape, while leaving spaces for greens to grow every-which-way. Generating material, then wielding an axe, leaves a view that I hope is valuable for having been made by someone who tripped over exposed roots under light filtered through green boughs. I don't want readers to feel lost in a forest, but I don't want them to be bored in a clear-cut either. The unknown can hold more wisdom than what seems certain.

My rough outline reminds me that there's something to keep moving forward to, while the path leaves room for new hills and hollows. I'm keeping a willingness to let the plot shift, let characters change before my eyes, swell from minor to major, or even disappear. My guide is a list of places that are important to my character, such as where she'll get angry, where she'll feel loss, where she feels safe, and where she feels in danger. This gives me direction while leaving spaces for the subconscious, or the part of me that's smarter than the one with colored pencils and a memory of triangles labeled with things like *rising action* and *climax*. Other questions include: Where does a road diverge and which way does she choose? Where does she feel most like what she calls herself? Where does she want to end up? Will she? These questions help me assess whether there's enough contrast in setting and accompanying feeling to create tension, and see whether my scenes have the necessary turning points.

I shuffle along with a ripped map and good-gripping sneakers. Stepping through puddles, brushing pine needles from my hair, and plucking prickers from my socks may mean I'm more likely to find a view nobody else has yet quite caught. Once I've collected material heading in all directions, I'm ready to sweep some into order and write *one, two, three*, and so on. But I keep in mind that people don't go into the woods, or read novels or poems, because they want clear signs. Readers like being a little bit lost, finding their own clues without the aid of neon markers. Finally, I cover up some tracks.

Chariots and Clouds

Peter and I were bicycling side by side this weekend when he brought up the first line of my work-in-process, which he'd recently read, and impressively quoted. "The mud-bricks under her bare feet hummed the way they did when chariots clattered toward the palace." He said, "I know you've never lived in a palace and I don't think you've ever heard a chariot, so how did you get that humming floor?"

"It's a kind of physical imagination," I replied. It's what we do in life when we exercise compassion, trying to feel ourselves into another person's life. I often write from the outside-in rather than staying stuck within a character's unclear heart or mind. What does she see, hear, smell, touch? Everything else may come to us as if glimpsed through a telescope, felt through mittens, or muffled by the bellows of an over-serious vocabulary. There's hardly a writer alive who hasn't been advised to show-not-tell. Most of us crave specifics such as the crunch of pomegranate seeds or the sting of a twisted ankle. We like the scent of an old creased love letter as much as the words. When I'm foiled by plot, I look, listen, or sniff around the rooms or land stored in my imagination. What kind of floor is under my protagonist's feet? What kind of table is under her pale brown hands? When researching a place that existed over four thousand years ago, I don't just study a picture of a chariot, but try to conjure the rumble it made on dirt roads, the scent of dust, and the way riders must have tensed their muscles to keep their balance between the wheels.

As I write, the present and past may collapse into one. Clouds like those above might once have drifted over the head of a girl who lived long ago. I'm not saying we should ever write, "It was a cloudy day." Particular descriptions of particular clouds may be too much. But it's good to at least imagine the sun's intensity, the shades of blue and white our characters walk under. Writing with an allegiance to what we see, words may reveal a pattern or detail, and we feel like a photographer who finds a bird, stone, or slant of sun that escaped her even as she framed the view.

I linger with a voice, place, or small objects until I understand not so much what they mean, but where they fit in a story that pulses and swells. The pull for a reader may be the question of what will happen next, a pull that may also get us to our work. My curiosity isn't particularly narrative, but poky and prone to dwell. So when inspiration gets ragged or rusty, as it's bound to do, I often return to objects, where an outer and inner world come together as they do in beloved faces we don't grow tired of looking at, wondering what's hidden and revealed by the eyes or the lines around the mouth.

We convince readers through details, but how do we know when we have enough? We need to immerse, but then select, so that each one not only makes readers feel as if they're part of the world we're making on paper, but also suggest a character's feelings and desires, perhaps ones she didn't know she had. We shouldn't cram a paragraph with objects, but scatter, choosing images that collide or mesh with underlying ideas. There's no need to show the whole closet. One unraveling mitten or the worn heel of a shoe may be enough. While I trim the text, I choose details that will stay because they contribute to a sense of characterization, theme, or setting, doing layers of duty. Some details were necessary to the creation, but if their power has faded, I whisper thanks while erasing them. Sometimes the power increases, and I'll repeat the imagery to amplify its effect, or fill the basements and attics of the houses I've created with simple objects that evoke mystery.

When a detail without an obvious purpose seems to insist on staying, I may look for different words for it, play with how I would describe it to someone who can't see or hear, or wrap it with associations it has for me. As I write freely, I sometimes stumble into a deeper meaning, and I understand not only why I want to but why I should keep the detail that first made me feel grounded, then rises slightly from the page. Here's an object I can unwrap, unwind, or unravel and find strands that fan out to suggest something beyond.

Starting with the senses can stir something hidden as surely as a cloth and polish can restore shine to tarnished silver. A spirit may seem to rise beyond the material, the way peeling paint may suggest the layers of history or the intricacies of a single bloom may summon possibilities beyond bouquets. The particular can seem what's most true, perhaps because it can't be contested. It may even swell into metaphor, which lets the concrete and abstract, the ordinary and grand, combine or collide. It's where we might leap from the small to large, and find meaning that may take years to unfold, the way fairy tales we loved as children glint with new possibilities when we're grown.

An object and meaning may become one, which some people call a totem or talisman, and others call a symbol, which is fine as long as that doesn't stir up bad memories from English classes, when symbol quests left out the delight of knocking into associations the way they should be found, with a film of dust or tarnish. A writer who chooses to leave in what might be called a symbol is not like a baker sneaking tofu into cake, sticking something good-for-you beneath the icing. A symbol should begin as a plain old thing, and sometimes that's where it will stay. We write first of the buttercup that's just a flower, and not a stand-in for innocence or cheer, the robin that's just a bird, not a harbinger of spring or messenger between earth and the heavens. But ordinary things might clothe the kind of secrets found in fairy tales where people are forbidden to speak certain names, fortunes, or fates. Revelations might be tucked within something as simple as eggs and flowers or thread and needles that can turn into cakes or dresses.

Meaning in life is usually at least half-hidden, and that's what we want when we write and read. We tend to trust whispers more than broadcasts. When we're lucky, something may unfold like an origami swan, slowing the pace with a glimpse inside paper wings, a lingering look at a long neck and dangly feet.

Beyond the Desk

_____

While doing errands in Amherst the other day, I ran into an illustrator who I see now and again, including at a book signing where, during one of the many lulls, he'd painted a small watercolor of my dog. When he asked, "How are things going?" I knew he meant what was happening on paper.

"Good. How about for you?" I replied.

His shoulders sank slightly as he told me how he'd thought he was 95% of the way through a picture book, but just got a note from the editor who informed him that instead there was quite a way to go. I commiserated, until he asked again about me, and I told him about my pleasure in creating a new draft of an old book.

He nodded. "I really needed to hear that. It's good to know that someone is happy in this business."

I think he was sincere, and didn't soon go on his way cursing me for flaunting contentment. There are days we all like to be reminded that sometimes things work out, and other days when even walking in the sun to a favorite library can't lift a sense of darkness. On afternoons when news of gorgeous books written by smart people can seem annoying instead of enticing, I stay at home rather than risk running into friends who might ask me when my next book is coming out, and I feel bound to stammer out a sentence shaped by evasions. On days like that, I might have left this colleague thinking, "Hey, you have an editor, a book coming out! Why should you complain?"

Somebody always has it better and somebody else always has it worse. We can get knocked down by jealousy, which loves a hierarchy, elbowing us to check out the other side of a table and mutter about unfair proportions on a plate. It's natural to feel twinges when some people seem to have consistently better luck, but before that green feeling spreads, it's good to remember that neither books nor joy are pies, and there's always room for more.

I don't mean to suggest I'm ever-balanced. Knowing that an editor I respect waits, although not in any day-counting sense, for a revision of my book about Enheduanna feels like a gift. But even when I'm in a less generous frame of mind, I try to remember that we who spend days with pen and paper or keyboards and screens have more in common than differences, and good fortune always has another side. Writers are on the same team, and cheering for each other on some days, commiserating on others, are one of the best parts of our work. Triumphs are rare enough that we're smart to celebrate each other's, and no one else understands quite so well what it's like to cope with stubborn silence at our desks or another kind of silence as we wait for responses from editors.

When I started mailing out manuscripts about thirty years ago, it was common to wait three months for a response. That's since doubled to six, and in many cases has doubled yet again. It's been over a year since I heard from an editor who'd asked for a revision of a picture book, and another editor I once worked with who has a novel supposedly under her consideration. Should I nudge them? I calculate the timing of conventions, spring and fall lists, tending to bigger books than mine, possible pregnancies or sick family members, vacations, and all the things that might get in the way of reading. I call this being considerate and patient, but it's also being scared to be considered a bother. I'm not pounding doors or following anyone into restrooms, just composing short, courteous emails. Sometimes hope is desperation in disguise.

In the years that I've sold eleven books, all directly to editors rather than through an agent, methods of communication have speeded up, but the estimated time in which we can expect to hear back has become longer. Form rejection letters have gone out of fashion in some quarters. Often now the protocol is that "no answer means no, thanks." There's a reason for this. Once upon a time, when editing was more central to an editor's job, and her decisions were given more respect within the company, there were fewer pieces to read. The Internet has made it easier for writers to find information about publishers and to send queries without printing out material, gathering and weighing envelopes, and calculating the price of stamps. This means more queries than many editors, agents, or their interns can find time to reply to. Writers are left to wonder if our words were ever read, lost, or glimpsed then forgotten because of more immediate concerns within the world of buy and sell. We scan incoming email feeling like the sad, nostalgic girl with her glass menagerie or a whaler's wife pacing the roof walk when no ship has been seen for a long, long time.

The business of publishing has always been hard. It's good to watch out for the warped truths of nostalgia, but I have rejection letters that seem almost quaint in that someone took the time to type, fold, and fetch an envelope, even if it was usually one I stamped and addressed myself. Receiving rejection letters often meant tears, though I was grateful for an occasional encouraging remark within them, and at least words on paper carried a sense that we shared a civilized business.

Silences and rejections make me lean on friends and family who help me channel discouragement into trying again, trying elsewhere, and writing something new. I may mutter, "They'll be sorry," to the dogs, and call up a story I heard about an editor who burst into tears while watching an author she'd turned down accept a major award. I expect this is, if not a myth, exaggerated, but fantasies don't have to be realistic to be satisfying. Sometimes I've imagined whole aisles of editors weeping.

I'm grateful for every editor who takes a risk, following her reader's heart. I understand all are doing their jobs, mandated to make or at least mind money, and perhaps uneasily aware that some writers are counting on book sales to pay the rent, too. Sadly, some such writers have turned to other work. The waiting is hard enough when one isn't counting on royalties for survival. I'm lucky to live on earnings from my husband's creative work, which had a Cinderella story aspect, a genre which finds its extreme in the saga of the single mom on the dole who wrote *Harry Potter and the Sorcerer's Stone* in coffee shops that were warmer than her flat. But we should remember that even Cinderella mostly wanted to dance. She wasn't counting on a castle. It's best to keep our daydreams smallish and our eyes mostly on our work, which can conjure gardens where transformations happen. There's richness and reward right there. Plenty of pumpkins for coaches or pie.

Our best choice is to keep writing in whatever way we do best, and valuing writer friends who are published and those who seem at varying lengths from that goal, which seems to slip in and out of reach. Sales are a risky measure of success. What matters most is what happens at the desk, where today I follow what intrigues me and try to tempt readers into intrigue, too. Soon I'll have to worry about how *Conversations with the Moon* will fare in the publishing world, but for now such thoughts only distract from what my best friends remind me is our work. Trying to make one small thing – our selves, a story – whole.

Sandcastles

Some of my friends are off to a big writing conference, where they'll sip lattes and listen to lectures that get their hearts racing. Meanwhile here I am at home, telling myself to listen up. Having two days pretty much to myself before my sister and her girls arrive for a visit, I decided to hold my own mini-conference on the screen porch. I'm serving blueberry iced tea and have stacked books by Laura Ingalls Wilder, Barbara Kingsolver, and Molly Peacock. I take a peek now and then, but mostly want the company at my elbow, with their promise of pleasure. The paperback covers curl in the heat.

I smell the freshly cut grass and rugosa roses beaten down by rain. Overhead, the sky is a steel gray. It's lonelier here than what my traveling friends will find, but there are no airport hassles. Parking is free! Pets are allowed! Maybe the food isn't the best, but neither is it the worst. No stale bagels, and we've got peas and basil from our friend Ed's garden for the salad. Around 8 a.m. we offer the fitness team of Mary with canines Parker and Millie; yesterday Mary insisted on three loops she now wants to call laps and warned me we might get back to four today. Other than that, it's a quiet conference. I'll miss laughing and discussing novels we've read or are writing, but the part of the process I'm in now asks for a quiet space to let a theme emerge.

Where is it? I try to make my way to the kind of silence where something entirely new arises, but it's not going well. The pines refuse to whisper answers. I can wiggle too much when I'm not starting something new or riding toward a visible end. I mutter. I yell at the dog (the cute one, who is loud). I want to shake the phone, willing it to ring, even if it's just a reminder about the dentist. I make more tea. Eat half a lemon bar. And get back to pushing around old phrases that don't sing. I'm tired of these people and this place. Can't my characters get themselves a little more together, please? Why can't a new and charming one show up? I call up the tried-and-true Dangling Carrot approach, reminding myself that local strawberries, an outing with Peter, and some swims are on the agenda. I mean to finish two pages, and when done, check what's happening online as a reward and begin again. No, maybe I'll check now.

I do away with some words that are quite lovely, but unfortunately don't quite fit. Then at last my characters become a little bit interesting again. For one moment I revel in all the words on the table. Being in the middle of a work is great! I might say there's a skeleton to my work, but that sounds creepy, or a map with roughed-out roads, but that makes it sound more structured than it is. Right now I'm thinking of my process as that of a kid who's piled up a lot of sand for a castle. Some sand will turn into turrets. Some will be shaped into windows. Some will be pushed down or collapse on its own. I explore, tear down, build another balcony.

I've still got to decide if I've left too many or not enough windows open. How many doors should there be, so readers can get in but not get lost? Decisions must be made, but right now it's more like play than work, even if, already wearing T-shirt and shorts, I don't look as serious as I'd like. Never mind. Sometimes there's seaweed and the sand looks kind of nasty. But something is better than nothing when it comes to castles or manuscripts, so it's okay to whine to myself, make peace with the dogs, maybe share the rest of the lemon bar with them, and see what I can find in the over-familiar characters.

Trouble

Sure, a writer's work and play are blended, but sometimes we have to put down the virtual shovel and bucket, put on a very virtual jacket and black pants, and get to serious work. Then later, take a serious break. When the porch gets really hot, I drive to the lake where I do lackadaisical laps past the raft, keeping an eye on children jumping off it. Twirling as they leap. Doing cannon balls. Twirling as they do cannon balls. I'm trying not to worry that one of them is bound to injure something. A lifeguard sits on the edge of the raft, spinning his whistle on its rope. He apparently believes they're safe.

When I write, I also hear my mom-voice, the one that wants to say things like: Please stop or at least watch your fragile heads. No one who's ever raised a child stops being a parent, but characters aren't our children. I struggle to keep the mom away from my desk where I'm writing about a girl who, like anyone, can't always wear her best clothes, hold her kindest expressions, and keep her bitter moments to herself. I've come to love this girl, and don't want her to go off in the woods alone. She should take my wise advice. But if she did, there wouldn't be much story. As a writer, it's best for me to be like the stepmother who sends children into the forest with stale bread and not even a reminder to keep away from witches and candy houses.

The parent who prays for only the sweetest things to happen has little place at a writer's desk. But love? Yes. The kind I'm trying to learn. Being there, but backing off when the time is right for a girl to choose paths I wouldn't consider and fulfill a destiny of her own.

I expect the lifeguard, staring through his sunglasses, spinning his whistle, would be a better sort of narrator than the safety-first mom who at her desk has a hard time making room for rough and wily antagonists, bullies, mean girls, dragons, or hard core villains. Characters should get in trouble. They should stumble all over themselves, collide into bad decisions and traps. But even more than the panicked mom or nonchalant lifeguard, I should stick with the children. Jumping with no thought of the future. Just a little reckless glee.

Is This a Beach or Is This a Joke?

I'm sitting on the porch, watching hummingbirds loiter
in their busy-winged way around the honeysuckle. The
sluggish cat is curled nearby, and the well-walked dogs are
panting. Peter is downloading photos, so there's a click-
click accompanying birdsong. He says, "You're sighing,
honey."

"Just organizational sighs. Part of the writing process."

He looks over to my computer and asks, "So when can
I read that book?"

"My goal is the beginning of September. It might still
be a bit rough, but …"

He nods, all too aware that I've been working on
Conversations with the Moon in various forms, with various
titles, stopping to tend to various other projects, for years,
and I'm never fast. Which is one reason why I like summer.
Heat makes me slow my pace, which matches my style of
writing. I'm fairly confident that this time through the
forward movement is vivid, though who can ever get
promises about roads that haven't yet been taken? It's all
word by word, page and page, with lots of hope thrown in.
And bumps.

Of which there are only so much you can take. There's
a fuzzy line between inspiration and procrastination. Taking
walks or reading books can both fuel ideas or steer us
around them. But when the clouds disappeared and I
decided to swim, I was pretty sure that was procrastination.
I want to write, but not with every joint creaking. I need to
move more than my fingers and elbows. Plus I got to see a
toddler in a pink bathing suit running in circles on the sand,
singing to herself.

Then when I was driving back down the dirt road away
from the water, a stranger flagged me down.

"I'm not from here," he said. As in *he-ah*. "I'm from
Texas, staying at the hotel ov-ah there. But I saw the sign
up there."

I nodded, glancing at the scrawled sign that says "Beach Open" under a picture of evergreens advertising "Xmas trees for sale." Which will be relevant again in six months.

"So is that a joke? Is there really a beach?" the man asked.

"It looks unofficial, but there really is a lake. It's just a few minutes walk."

"I thought it might be a joke," he repeated, then walked on while I drove away from the lovely lake that lets me float on my back and reminds me that it's good to spend some time staring at the sky.

I'm thinking that when I tell Peter that really, truly I'll have a draft of my novel by the end of August, I don't want him saying, "Is this a joke?" Not that he would. But I don't want my promise to look like a hand-scrawled sign. I want him to be sure that there really is a lake.

Other Living Rooms and Porches

When I told Mary that I'd be heading to a lake house soon to write among friends, she said, "You're pretty disciplined about writing. So why do you need a retreat?"

I explained that even before I leave home for a few days, I write with more vigor, having decided what I want to work on while away and making sure that section is ready. Ideas often arrive in new ways when I'm working with a view of writers' shoulders bent over laptops or hands shuffling colorful index cards to lay out a plot. A day devoted to writing fills with all its rhythms: one minute I have a terrific answer, the next I'm not so sure, and the next I skip from despair to plodding along. While away, I drop a few procrastinating habits and hope some will stick, the way I hope that when I return home the little dog will be out of his habit of wanting a snack at four a. m. There's a little fantastical thinking going on here, but the pleasure of sitting in the midst of creative people at computers stays with me for a good long time. And when I revise words I wrote while looking out an unfamiliar window, sometimes I get to recall views of water.

Retreats don't have to be highly organized events, but may be a few days holed up alone or with a friend or two. I love visiting my grown daughter in LA, where after she leaves for work, I may set up my laptop, eat cereal from a zebra-print bowl, throw in some laundry, and break to walk to get coffee in a shop where everyone's sandals are more glittery than mine. Along the way, I get great whiffs of eucalyptus.

Sometimes I meet friends to write for a few hours, which changes the routine and breaks up the long hours of being alone. One afternoon Peg and I met at our friend Michelle's house, where she'd set out a pretty pitcher of iced tea with sprigs of mint.

"I remember coming to your house, and you always put mint from your garden in the tea," she told me. "So I did, too."

I'd gotten out of that practice, which she'd carried on. Mint's cool green leaves, that light scent, were just what my work-in-progress, which had been feeling a bit too dark and heavy, needed.

This is one reason why we meet. To remind each other of what one of us offered at one time, and to be offered back in turn. To be reminded, really, of everything.

Retreat

———

After greetings in the inn perched among pines, I settle in with my laptop and type, glancing up at Lake Champlain. At the end of the afternoon, I gather with about twenty-five other writers on the porch, where we sip wine and talk about what we hope to accomplish over two days: Are forty pages possible? Confronting an event remembered from decades back? Figuring out how to plot a mystery? Finishing a novel's revision, or at least a chapter? Why not? Then there was dinner, more laughter, and more writing in a main room that is both elegant and cozy.

Getting ready for bed, my roommate asks, "Did you have a productive evening?"

"Um, something got done."

"You were tearing up some pages pretty definitively."

"Yeah, I can tear up pages with confidence."

The next morning begins with yoga led by a young woman who puts about half of our group through sun salutations, down dogs, tree poses, and hard stuff that isn't part of my gentle yoga class at the library. Then she says, "*Namaste*. Go. You're really just going to write all day? Really? Write? All day?"

Yup. All days have twenty-four hours, but they seem longer when unbroken by chores, diversions, or much talking. When the day is devoted to writing, time moves as slowly as the sun. In an unbroken afternoon, my characters relax and tell the kind of tales you get when there are no buses to catch, no phones that might ring, when they know they've got my attention. They stutter less and speak whole sentences at a time.

I work through the morning, while a simple lunch is being prepared for us, leaving no excuse for wondering things like if the lettuce has gone by, and should I check and perhaps drive to the farm stand? We could take a sandwich elsewhere and keep writing, but most chose to share tables where we talk about things like favorite first lines or the small friendly pressure of writing in company.

Most agree that pressure is good, as long as it doesn't push us into the realm of scaring ourselves. Some feel that talking about a piece can bring energy, while others find talking is more apt to make the work disappear.

Soon we get back to placing our fingers over keyboards and gazing at water. Around me, some writers are putting characters in peril. My hope was to write a poem, holding myself as steady as a fisherman throwing out a net, then keeping my hands still. The net may widen or sink, billow or bunch up, but the good fisherman keeps his feet steady and tosses the net again.

I fail to catch a poem, but collect about eleven pages of flotsam and jetsam. Stuff that isn't poetry, but might make its way into some. And I'm happy to net what looks like a usable metaphor.

The next day, rain keeps the temptations of boat rides and swimming at bay. Where do ideas come from? The vast gray lake, the loons, the spruce trees, the quiet company settled in a row of wicker chairs on the porch, somewhere deep inside? I take my place in one of those chairs, listen to the soft sounds of rain on the water, watch two intrepid boats drift around an island. Then I dive into a day of words. I heard a legend or gossip that someone figured out a key piece of her book while sitting by some flat rocks near the water, and rain or not (I've got an umbrella), I'm getting there this afternoon.

On the last night we sit on the porch and everyone describes what they accomplished that day. Someone remembered a haunting relationship, which she knew it was time to face. Someone else wrote five chapters. Another woman cut the last words of some chapters. Someone else made rhymes. If a writer did well, she (or a lone he) was adorned with a lei. We all got one.

The Long View

I balk at writing a synopsis when a book is finished, squishing all my work onto a page or two jammed with abstractions. But I find that pausing midway to write a rough draft of what-happens-and-what-it's-about may show me whether I'm hitting what I hope to hit. After peering so long at the small picture, straightening up to look at the big one helps me see if I'm going in a good direction. Telling the main story in a few quick breaths can help me determine if the details and dialogue I'm compiling will contribute to what's essential.

So I just whipped off a page stating what my manuscript is about. The good news is that it's about something. Or it will be. The bad, if unsurprising, news: we aren't getting there fast enough. So I'm back to trying to make sure each chapter addresses the main crisis and moves with the right amounts of smoothness and tumult to the next. I'm reminded to make sure something may be lost or won, something is at risk, even if it's not as fraught as the hobbits Tolkien has make through their way through dangerous forests toward a dragon. An ax hovers over all of *Charlotte's Web*. The White Witch can appear anytime in Narnia and turn anyone to stone. I'm writing about a young woman whose concerns aren't matters of life and death or stone, but sometimes a wrong word or two can feel that way. Dragons, an ax, a soul at peril, all cast shadows.

Writers must spend a lot of time with our noses close to manuscripts, but we need to survey how all the scenes fit together not only when starting out, or even heading toward an end, but every once in a while. We're like painters, careful about the spots where our brushes touch canvas, but often stepping back to see how one color contrasts or blends with another, how each shape affects those beside it. Writers should look up from the sentences under our fingertips and check for a sturdy plot and a structure that doesn't wobble. This is also like life, which we mostly live day by day, but taking an occasional long look back or forward may smarten up our next steps.

The other morning when Mary and I walked our dogs through the woods, she mentioned a study done by scientists on perception. They reported that some people may see just a field, while others, say those who study butterflies, focus on milkweed and other plants that provide food for the insects. I like to fiddle with the tiny parts of my writing, which isn't useful as I consider the shape of a whole book. Finding my way through its thorny middle, I note the weeds, brambles, slugs, and signs of ticks. Then I stop, unbend, stretch, and keep my eyes wide open for the spacious view.

Bravery and White Space

I just gave Peter some poems to read. He had comments about this or that word choice, and some reservations about the tense I chose, but his most meaningful comment was the charge to tell a little less. The way he put it was to have confidence in the story, and to cut words that were explanatory. That is, get rid of my signposts that indicated: *Important news ahead! Pay attention!* or *In case you didn't know …*

Could I do without these markers? Readers have imaginations, and it's good to let them work. I hit delete here, and there, and still another there. I think the work survived.

Writing is full of these breath-catching pauses, like the kind we wait for in a conversation, offering a chance to change or deepen the subject. How much can we take out and still make just enough sense? How much can we peel away, while leaving a sense of the moment that first engaged us? I've long thought of paring as essential to my writing, but I hadn't thought about it in terms of courage. It's not a word I usually apply to soft-spoken me who prefers watching from sidelines to scuffling in a field. Yet every phrase we pluck may make us more light-headed. We want to leave something for readers to grab onto, but also spaces where they can do their own wondering and make the words their own. Sometimes we want to hear every word of a conversation, and sometimes it's enough to hear only the slap of sandals on stone or frogs calling from the marsh.

Sharks in the Kitchen

Back in my too many years as an English major, with college stretching for reasons beyond the fact that it took me a while to master the concept of requirements, I was crazy about Virginia Woolf and took on a certain amount of her disdain for plot. I had time and patience, and could happily read hundreds of pages in which not very much happened. When I started writing short stories, Alice Munro was my model. Who could ask for more than two women reminiscing at a kitchen table?

I've always liked books that proceed at a leisurely pace and am fond of the word "quiet." But seeing that word in a rejection letter makes me get pretty loud. So I've revived my respect for plotting, looking at my manuscript for places I can put in secrets, and the sorts of drama I try to avoid in my life. When I tell Peter that I'm trying to build action, he's quick to suggest monsters, blizzards, sandpits, sharks, tornados, extraterrestrial attacks etc. Thanks, honey. Maybe I should listen, or to someone I recently heard talk about how trying to write quiet prose was not going to get anyone far in publishing, because readers today are noisy, multi-tasking, all-over-the-place, and want writing that reflects their busy, perhaps even frenetic, states of mind.

I don't know. We are who we are, and it shows up on our pages. I was a quiet child and when I became a writer, that restraint came into my work. We can accept, and some days even treasure, who we are, but sometimes we should tramp into new territory and aim for different notes, volumes, and rhythms. I find my character tipping, when she can use a good push. Or raising her eyebrows when she needs to slam her fist.

Many years ago, I took a dance class that the teacher said was inspired by African, Caribbean, jazz, modern dance, and her cat's stretches. In one class, as I raised a leg and leaned into what I thought was an arabesque, Diana yanked on my foot, pulled my arms, tipped me almost over, and said, "You think you're moving when you aren't."

The words stuck not because I was to go on with dance – I was there for the fun, art, and exercise – but because they summed me up. I'm not going to put sharks in my kitchens, but I want to keep readers turning pages. So I try to stretch. There's Diana, laughing, reminding me that I can skip or slide a little further.

Metaphors by my Elbow

I was making headway through a chapter, then stumbled during a last lap. But I got back on track, and could see the finish line getting nearer. Hmmm. I'm not a runner, but sports metaphors slip in when I want to connect my writing process with one that has more color or action. I once saw a recorded interview with Eudora Welty taken in her gracious Southern home. She stepped around a dining room table covered with stacks and single sheets of papers. In her lovely accent, she said that plotting was just like cutting out a dress. I, too, like to move papers around, and once upon a time made dresses from fragile paper patterns I pinned to cloth set on a dining room table. So as I write, I sometimes think of stages of dressmaking, from pattern-laying, to snipping, to sewing seams, then the triumphant final hemming.

Other times in my teens, I'd gently set the stereo needle on a vinyl record to hear Laura Nyro's *Stoney End* or James Taylor sing *You've Got a Friend*. The needle on the black disc sometimes comes to mind when I feel words fall into place. I'm all for new technology, but I wonder if my writing would be different if I didn't have the memory of setting down a needle as I touch a pen point to paper, inviting words to spin around.

Nature also gives us ways to mirror both stories and our process as we put them on paper. In *The Writing of Fiction*, Edith Wharton compares the parts of a novel to an ocean wave. She wrote that exposition should be most of the wave, while dialogue was its dramatic peak. This worked in her fiction, though few of us today would choose the same balance. I'm not even sure she did, but her point was that dialogue gives the power, and perhaps should be used more sparingly than we first think. So much of a wave leads up to a peak, but some well-chosen words within quotes can make everything curl over.

I like thinking of writing in terms of bodies of water. I recently looked at a picture Peter took of the river that goes along a favorite bike path in Turners Falls. The reflections, even though blurred, are as stunning as the bank of flowers. I don't want my words to run into each other, but the photograph suggests to me that some might be better off in the background, becoming the rising wave rather than its crest. I'm considering what words should recede and which should stand in front.

Who Takes Her Computer on Vacation?

I'm packing bathing suits, towels, sunscreen, bug repellant, and too many books, getting ready to head for the Maine coast, near where Peter and I got married, and where we've been vacationing since soon after Emily was born. Pat, who's getting a break in her chemo treatments, which she's decided to take as a good sign, will stay with us most of the two weeks. Her husband, Ed, and Peter will take time off from work for a few days. Other friends and relatives will come and go. We see some on holidays, which get jammed, not to mention stressed, so it's nice to have days when the questions are: Which beach should be go to? Which movie should we watch? Want some more iced tea?

Before I left, Mary asked me if I wrote on vacation. I explained that I find time in the morning, since I'm often awake before anyone thinks of swimming or moving beyond the porch. And maybe I'm a little superstitious about bringing a project to a long halt. Would I be able to begin again, or get addicted to a different pace? Would my characters pack up and leave? Fear motivates, but it's also simply pleasant to write in a different spot than usual. Words don't always come straight from mind to hands, and in coffee shops, I've seen writers like me look past their computers and tilt their heads like robins searching for worms on lawns. Then we pounce. By the ocean, while considering a phrase, I get to gaze at blue or gray.

Morning light slants into the bedroom from two sides, flickering off a huge and ragged old birch, while an unfamiliar bird chirps. I head downstairs and take my place on the porch, which is close enough to the shore to hear waves splash on rocks. Peter and Emily are late nighters and late sleepers. Pat, like me, gets up early, but she's content to watch the sun follow its course, hear water lap and pages turn. She whispers, "J, do you want tea? Sorry, sorry to interrupt."

"I'm set for now, thanks. It's all right." In fact,

everything's perfect. I'm wearing t-shirt, shorts, and a shabby sun hat. My feet are bare and I've got a grocery list in my pocket. Sometimes I watch a chipmunk scurry, his mouth filled with a tomato-red rosehip. A dragonfly flits by. And there's the ocean. Waves splash silvery spray.

And there's the clock. I'm not going to say I don't peek at it, wondering when it's time to head off with loved ones and get battered by waves and sand, take calmer swims in a lake, or eat fried clams or fish. Meanwhile I'm practicing stillness, slowly searching for elusive words while watching the air change colors over stones.

I'm trying to assume the pace of a sailboat, not a motorboat or even a kayak. A fisherman in an orange jacket stands in a bobbing white boat. I'm sitting still on a wicker chair with my laptop on my lap, but I feel as if I'm bobbing too. I watch him throw out a line, risk his balance. Sometimes the world offers us a rhythm. Wave, wave, wave. And sometimes we have to create one ourselves. Sit, sit, sit. There's a conversation between us and the part of the earth where we choose to be, with every wave a new chance and an invitation to write. Gentle, rushy sounds keep me company. One could forget everything else here, and for a while, I do. Is that poetry I hear stirring? Maybe.

Gathering

So I had this lovely fantasy of having some writing friends visit our rented house tomorrow. Pat said she'd be happy to catch up on reading, and Emily tends to sleep through most of the morning. So my friends and I could write and eat lunch to the civilized sound of waves. Now I just heard from a friend who thought that instead of coming with his partner on the weekend, it would work better to arrive tomorrow. Okay. Then ten minutes ago, Emily told me that three of her friends are on their way up, didn't she tell me? Not exactly. And Pat isn't feeling that well. Thunder rumbles and more storms are predicted.

"Where will everybody sleep?" I asked Emily.

"Mom, we'll work it out. And we've got chocolate fondue."

"Oh, I bought strawberries."

"Good! We forgot about something to dip."

So I'm baking brownies and starting a chicken salad and hoping the dog behaves and the morning has a little peace for my friends to write. These are the lessons we're supposed to keep learning, right? Nothing is perfect. Go with the flow. Hey, there's an ocean out there! Chill.

Can I? Well, the brownies are starting to smell good.

Then my writer friends arrive. We admire the ocean, complain a few complaints, cheer good news and cross fingers for more. I find an extension cord for the four laptops and we all write on the screened porch. Emily and her friends quietly carry late breakfasts to the deck, and if Nell chose peanut butter ice cream cake for hers, well, it's vacation. The thunder holds off long enough for the girls to get to the beach. When our writing is done, Pat joins us for lunch and a short walk past daisies and pink roses to the rocky shore. We share her ritual of tossing in stones and making a wish.

As the writers leave, my other friends arrive. For supper, we go out for Mexican food. Sounds pretty perfect, yes? It gets even better. When I turn out the lights downstairs and head to my bedroom, I find Pat sitting up in her bed writing. Was it my friends tapping on computers this morning, the ocean, or the margaritas that inspired her to pick up a pen? Maybe all of the above. Many people have told Pat that she should write a book about how she's coped with lupus, which was diagnosed shortly before I met her about twenty-five years ago, and learning she had cancer. I suggested she start off by writing about one afternoon, or one conversation. Busy with so many other things, Pat hadn't taken out paper until last night when she wrote nine pages. She told me she focused on an afternoon at the cancer center, which she'd told me about earlier. It was an afternoon when truth made some of her hope split. Or that crack let in another kind of truth.

This morning I get back to writing on the porch, feeling the ghostly glow of friends who sat where I sit now, wishing I knew what wonderful words they typed here, but willing to wait and see.

Back Home

I'm no longer there to hear or smell it, but I'm glad to know that the ocean keeps doing its ocean thing. Clams keep getting fried. Back in Massachusetts, I'm starting to see signs of fall. At the local farm stand, I still find zucchini, peaches, and blueberries, though they're wrinkled. Apples and pumpkins are for sale, too. Am I ready for them? No. I stick to corn that's not as sweet as it is in July. But maybe next time I'll buy a bag of Macs or Cortlands, and consider the chrysanthemums.

On my porch, it's no longer so hot that I have to shoo off the cat slathered over my laptop. The crickets make a racket. The hydrangeas are turning pink at the edges. Yesterday was the last day that our local beach was open. A lifeguard dragged in the buoys, while I swam back and forth, mentally revising a few sentences I'd written that morning. Children wearing hats made of more fabric than their bathing suits toddled to the water to fill pails. Bigger children stalked the shore with nets or shovels. Some dug holes. Some sat in holes.

Except for the disappearing buoys, there was no sign that most of us won't smell sunscreen for a while and we're leaving the water to the geese and occasional herons. No one gave speeches about the last swimming day of the year. I didn't hear anyone call good-bye to the lake. There were no declarations, a reminder to me who loves to tie up stories with bright bows or tug the end of a verse into a fancy shape. Sometimes just stopping is the best way to end.

I'm seeing my way through this revision of *Conversations with the Moon,* whose ending is not exactly a mirage, but does shift in and out of sight. As I cross out lines, I feel a pinch in my throat. It's difficult to know just what to leave out, trusting readers to make leaps and savor uncertainty. There are bound to be cracks between what is seen and what's recorded. Peter remembered this while sketching rocks by the shore: that realization that what's drawn is never what's before us. And that's all right. One makes lines to suggest. The world is inspiration, and art is not a mirror. Imagination, like dreams, is uneasy with boundaries. The places where borders break may be the places where someone strikes out on a journey or a stranger comes to town, and another story begins.

Dodging and Digging a Way
Toward Theme

When people ask about our inspiration, they want to know what drew us to a subject, but that may be something we only uncover while making our way through several drafts. Remembering or finding why our subject seemed to call may help us go wider or deeper, following a link that goes back farther than we thought, and which may serve as a guide to suggest what details belong and what can be put away. Writing the middle of a manuscript, we may discover what matters most.

Theme appears after a lot of work. Beginning with an idea may be setting out from the wrong end. I like to start with the small, the way carpenters begin with a few nails and a board or a cook with a fork and a fistful of eggs. A single correct note can lead into an opera. We need a slender needle and thread before we get a wedding dress.

Like the best questions, themes sprawl or stay as hidden as a heart. Theme doesn't like a starting point or even a straight track and certainly not a timer. Themes tangle, twist, and even thwart, asking writers to trace back our steps and find new ways in. Maybe themes aren't like kudzu, but like geraniums allowed to stretch far from the rim of a pot. Theme can be sticky, prickly, or murky, so writers look for what not only acknowledges but stirs up rough patches. We find themes only after we've created a place for them to grow, then may look back for signs of them that should remain half-hidden. Most readers want thoughts that move like fables, going from the particular to the general.

What preoccupies us may influence how our characters think and speak. The mothers and daughters in *Borrowed Names,* six people who aren't much like me, were developed not only through my research, but also tensions I'd felt as a daughter and a mom. What we call obsessions in life might be called themes when turned to stories. These rarely race to find us, but are more likely to slide in, swerve, sprawl, snake, trip or slow us down. Understanding doesn't happen in a flash. That's why we're given lifetimes for it. After multiple drafts of exploring the nitty-gritty, we may stumble into theme, which leaves tracks that needn't and shouldn't be named. If this knocks us off our timetables, it's best to change the timetable. We don't want to fritter away time, but good listening requires stillness, a sense that whispers can connect us more than shouts.

Learning how to let words thicken with meaning comes from both life and practice. I'm sometimes asked whether I think the art and craft of writing can be taught. Yes, of course, though my way is mostly to encourage moving hands, staying alert for gifts or missteps and ways those can be the same, and finding friends who will cheer along the way.

Some people make learning to write more complicated. Back in college, I took a class for those of us planning to teach high school English. Our professor used long, flavorless words and stressed scientific studies. He presumed that the writing process could be explained, measured, and packaged to pass along, while my own experience was of rough edges and bonny surprises.

One afternoon he asked us to write a paper with violence as the theme. The topic seemed pulled from a list meant to provoke well-crafted paragraphs, perhaps with secondhand opinions about violence in video games or the movies. He suggested we could analyze gun laws or urban statistics. He loved statistics. The assignment seemed designed for us to start with generalizations and stay there, and presumed we should ask the same of students we'd soon teach. Would I be doomed to reading stacks of papers filled with arguments lifted from other opinion pieces? I wasn't particularly a fan of Kafka, but whatever happened to wanting to write like an ax for the frozen seas within us?

Also, I was furious. The abstract word stirred painful memories I couldn't fit into a paper, especially one I'd hand to a man I didn't much like or trust. Looking back, I'm more forgiving of the assignment and the assigner. I'm certain I've asked students to do more obnoxious things. I suppose he hoped to see movement toward something grand, and was perhaps unaware that many of us need a grittier place to start. Some professors find it hard to ask people to write about a pebble, feather, or even a pond, though we know Thoreau found a way to say everything he knew about life, which was a great deal, starting from a one-room cabin with a view of water. None of this occurred to me as I struggled with how I was going to do the assignment, get the damned grade I wanted, and stay true to myself.

Determined to keep allegiance to my senses, I wrote about a recent evening when I drove a borrowed car through falling snow and growing darkness, using directions that included turns at stonewalls and apple orchards. I recognized the gnarled, gray branches, and found the small house on a hill, which seemed a place where one could hide or heal. I wrote about the scent of cups of tea made by an old friend from high school, a loom by the woodstove, burning a bit too high, a waiting bassinet, and the sounds of Scrabble tiles as we laid them down on the pine table, finally leaving some scattered, rather than going on to see which of us might win or lose. Sue and I didn't say much, but we listened deeply, sensing the hard memories behind our soft words. I turned what was supposed to be an essay with a presumably authoritative tone into a narrative with a shaky first person voice.

I kept to the edges of the particular violence we each endured when we were eighteen, as I do here, for the ways we recognize each other as people who've felt split in two, trying to dodge a past that has surely shaped us, is a topic that demands to go not only beyond a word but an essay. Some of us who were told, "Don't tell," later push against that threat, trying to tell on paper what we left behind and the ways we've remade ourselves. Violence may have turned me into more of a writer. And there's that word again. Do I sound contradictory to insist that it's bleached-out when it set off a response like a knife between my ribs? What mattered was not its confined sound, but my angry response to it, which prodded me back to the physical world, calling up what was and releasing it in words.

Writing can be grieving. Acknowledging one small thing after another was the slow, unsteady way I learned to look back at what I didn't want to remember. I felt like a victim while being told to call myself a survivor. That was one more thing I could blame myself for. I couldn't shake my fear and shame until I spoke and wrote about what had happened, using many words to find my way to ones that showed me my own strength.

Reading, and exchanging shy and knowing glances, taught me that what had left me achingly lonely was in fact a common story. We plan our lives, but we become who we are in between what we want and what we get, in the collision and climbing out. Laying out a book happens similarly. We draw up plots, but if we're willing to let things stay rough for a while, making outlines that we're willing to tear, we may stir mysteries that lead to new connections. The words we choose and change may reveal what we didn't know we knew.

That's one reason why I write. Even as I create new characters or research people from history, I discover links between who I am now and who I used to be. I work my way through obsessions, fears, anger, and yearnings for justice through stories that start small. I find words for memories that I once couldn't tell, but needed to, because untold stories shape us.

As I found themes in the lost voices of women, I never forgot the divided girl I was at eighteen or the shy, freckled nine-year-old with pointy glasses. Everyone I used to be is part of me. And if you count imagination, which I do, I'm also all the people who I've spent time with on paper. I once was a girl watching dragonflies, calling out for someone to look. I lived about four thousand years ago and left home to find a new one, using a stylus to set my thoughts into clay. I'm a lucky person.

Fall: Revising

Revising doesn't mean turning at the last page and getting out highlighters, red pens, brooms, or hatchets. I'm pretty much revising all along, wrangling an idea into a sentence, trying out a rhythm, and ripping apart paper to be sure I'm not tempted to track down places for what doesn't belong. Toward the end of a book, I do a lot of sawing, but stop to rebuild, too. And once in a while I catch sight of sturdy walls and a solid roof.

The Goddess Kali at the Computer

I trust in the revision process to find what's amiss, including tired images that need to be woken up or the missing sound of a beating heart. I'm prepared to clip away scenes that are limp or lusterless, to clear a path for something that rises and falls in a satisfying way. I straighten up, then toss words to the wind. Playing with what's scattered, and seeing how some words look when propped against different ones, I make new connections. Holes demand to be filled. The more of a mess I make at this stage, the likelier I am to push the story to the next level. It's like cleaning out a closet. While everything's still on the floor, even if organized into piles, it all looks more cluttered than ever. I'm tempted to cheat, shoving some things in trash bags, sticking the rest in any old vacant place. I strive to be patient with chaos, giving myself time to spot words that will settle comfortably side by side or startle.

Making something and letting it go can happen in less than a minute. A student in my writing class is also an illustrator, and when I recently brought in colored pencils, she asked, "Where are the erasers?" She said that she always drew with an eraser in her other hand, which now opened and closed around nothing. This reminds me of how I forget how close the delete button is to my pinky. It reminds me of Kali, the Hindu goddess of destruction and creation, who invites the new by clearing out the old.

As I revise, I imagine wearing plaid flannel, rugged trousers, hip boots, and a hat with a net to keep off insects that might storm from the hacked-away underbrush. But there's a time to stash the axes under the tea table, lest flying grasses scare off new ideas that may rise from the thatch. Three days ago I had an idea that still makes my eyes shine. I told Peter, around four in the afternoon, about an hour before I had to leave the house, that I was going to my writing room to write, not delete. And I did.

Yesterday I let more words stay than I struck out. I

don't know what I'll get today, but I do know that I have to write a lot of flat or just plain bad scenes before a plot snares or sparkles. I study pages to see if they just need housekeeping. Should I ask characters to pick up their feet or elbows while I sweep or dust? Or should I offer new chances for them to get a little wild, try a different city or company, or get lost? Maybe. For now, I'll let one of my favorite goddesses kick whatever's in her way and swing sharp objects, so she will be my friend.

The Place We're Supposed To Be

It's the season when pumpkins sit on porch steps and sacks of candy corn and gummy bats fill store shelves. The hydrangeas I planted a few years ago first turn cream-colored, then rosy, and finally a golden-brown. If the deer don't eat off their tips, they'll bloom again next year. The crickets are getting louder. Goldenrod is taking over the meadows. There's nothing like fall foliage to remind you to seize the day. Except perhaps a dog, for whom every walk is as good as the last one and better than the next.

When I began writing in my twenties, it was to kind of to save my life. I had feelings I hardly dared to put in words and kept my notebooks secret. Then I worked up the courage to enroll in writing classes where stories were set on a table surrounded by eleven other writers. I was careful about what I typed onto what some of you may remember as carbon paper to make duplicates. Before I showed my work, I had to believe that it was as good as it could be at the moment, that it was both mine and would be worth the time someone might take to read it.

I'm still cautious about the early drafts I show to people. My writing group is willing to look at anything, but I want what they read to have gone through my own interior cycles of compression and shaking out. I catch edges of poems that look tarnished. Can magic really rise from the mundane? Every time I tell myself to go back for another round, I sigh. But soon enough – no, never soon enough – I see: This is better than what I did before.

Still, it's not perfect. Nothing is. Or so we've been told, or said, maybe when somebody was whining. I remind myself that perfection, or its approximation, rises from dust, sweat, and muck, and those will leave traces. It's a gift to think something isn't done yet, for that stance can show how much we value excellence. But it can be a trap, too. A time comes to shrug off standards that are impossibly high instead of just high. We must learn to trust our own sense of when we're ready to take another leap of faith into new work.

I suppose life would be easier if someone else could tell us when we're on the right or wrong track. One of my writing students recently asked me if I thought she had talent or if she should give up. She'd been noticing that others seemed more confident of their visions and voices, and wondered if she might be a fraud to even attempt to keep up. Did I have advice?

I write, teach writing, and occasionally review books, so it's not altogether surprising someone might think I could tell the difference between a real writer and someone who's faking it. But I didn't have a clue. I assured her that wondering if your words have any value, or feeling surrounded by people who seem more secure, can hit any of us at any time. Such feelings are part of moving into new and rocky territory. Fear is part of the process, often accompanied by questions such as: Why can't I write faster? Couldn't thirty-seven instead of thirty-nine revisions be enough? Why does everyone interrupt me? Why does everybody leave me alone?

Maybe every college should offer courses in Insecurity 101 or Advanced Anxiety. Breaking through doubts is what happens in the corridors with classmates, in hallways at writer's conferences, or over cups of coffee with friends. We find consolation among others who've also survived harsh critiques or rejections, check in and decide how much crying is too much. How do we separate criticism of our work from criticism of our selves? It's always about the work, and always feels personal, so I advise muttering, endangering no life forms, and getting a good night's sleep. And you may have picked up how much I love my dogs.

Recently, Peter asked me if I thought I was writing better. The question kind of stopped me, so I stalled by saying, "Well, I don't think I'm getting worse."

Writing the best I can in a given moment takes all my focus, and I'm not keen to look back to compare. But, yes, practice has made me grow more comfortable with language. Words flutter forth more easily, never mind how many I still swat down. I'm quicker to toss what seems witty but not wise, what's perhaps worthwhile but not of a front row seat. My mind feels pretty well-flexed, the way my body feels after a good yoga session: I'm glad to stretch toward another word or change the syntax, just as I'd twist my elbow in another direction. Sometimes I even believe that I'm exactly where I'm supposed to be.

Looking for Last Lines

Poetry may let both writers and readers see the world differently. As we swap old names for feelings, or worn stories about our lives for new images, we can change our vision. That's why I have little patience for those who don't believe in revising poetry, though it should be done with care not to let the small flames that began them flicker out. This week, I'm looking for the right words to end not only poems, but a collection with a narrative thread I've kept running through about 150 pages. Each time through I sit longer with each line of each poem, hoping to make it not only shiny in itself, but a steppingstone to the next.

Since my poems usually start as pictures in my mind, moving away from imagery and playing more with sound can lead me to last lines that include traces of something both old and new. Or I may switch from thinking of what I do as writing to look for parallels in music, art, dance, or another form less wed to literal meaning. Is the rhythm right? Is the weight too wispy or too heavy? Is there an intriguing shift in colors?

Reading other people's poems can unfasten me from my own predictable ways, fling me into a dizzy state good for this stage of revising. I may simply enjoy another's voice or I may pay attention to various strategies for ending. Did the poet land on an image, forge a latch that clicks into place? Does the view widen with questions or get smaller? If we tend to end with something small or concrete, it can be good to try pulling out the rug and end with something grander, though probably not a view of the sky or a short lecture. We can shift the point of view from one side of the room to the other or from overhead to closer to the ground.

Setting a question or two in my mind, then taking a walk or a nap, usually works better than seeking an answer by chewing a fingernail and staring at the page. Will I end with dialogue or description, a character's action or proclamation? Is there a clue to the ending in my title or in the first stanza? Instead of circling back to tag the first line, maybe I should abruptly cut the rope. I've often lopped off some lines and found mystery and resolution curling together buried just a little bit back.

Is each poem complete, or did I simply not know where to go next? I wish writing poetry were more like baking. I set the timer and eventually the cake will rise, though there are always a few adjustments: slipping in a knife to tell if it's still sticky inside or pressing with my fingertip to see if the surface bounces back. At least we know what a cake is supposed to look and taste like. Poetry is trickier. Recently someone sent me a poem, asking for my opinion. I told her I liked it, but mentioned a few words and phrases that felt a bit mushy. The poet agreed, then emailed me back her revisions, to which I gave my blessing. A few hours later, she sent another slightly revised version. Then another, with a few words changed. I've been asked to do this sort of instant editing before, and find it impossible to judge at such close range. I told her that the poem was hers now. She didn't have to, and shouldn't, stop playing or wrestling with it. But besides the editing difficulty of seeing slight shifts, there's a time to offer your poem to critique and a time to own it.

We work in a field with no finish lines, so we make our best guesses as to when to let a poem rest, then come back with fresh eyes. If the poem can surprise me, or if I sense that the words were already tossed and shaken, that's a good sign. Words should follow each other in clear ways, but leave some sense of an imperfect hand doing the arranging and room for readers to do their own shuffling.

At last I say good-bye for now to a river across the world, where long ago the clay along its banks was used to make pots, bricks, and writing tablets that endured. I'm sending out my book about Enheduanna, reminding myself that anything can happen, but I can't help daydreaming about an enthusiastic email – will it come within a week? a month? – congratulatory hugs from friends, and a party where I'll serve dates, salty cheese, flat bread, olives, and pomegranate martinis.

By the River

Purple loosestrife brightens the edges of the highway as I drive east to meet a friend in a Concord coffee shop. Amy and I eat muffins, write, and take breaks to talk about our families and the books we're completing. We walk from town to the river, turning at the Old Manse where Nathaniel Hawthorne and his wife lived after they were first married, where he wrote fiction, Sophia painted, and in the summer they tended to a garden that had been planted by Henry David Thoreau as a wedding present. Amy and I pass beanpoles, dried corn stalks, and lolling cabbages. Stopping by the bridge and a statue that marks the American Revolution, I talk about Louisa Alcott and my interest in her youngest sister. May painted throughout her life, not stopping upon discovering that she wasn't a genius, as Louisa had the sister based on her do in *Little Women*. Amy tell me how much she dislikes that message that passions aren't worth following unless they result in masterpieces, prizes, or acclaim. It's sad to see young people stop dancing, drawing, playing baseball, or writing stories, abandoning what they love to those with more perceived talent.

The river softly laps stones. Fallen leaves, smelling like slightly burning toast, crunch under our feet. This is not just the place where the British fled from Minutemen, but where girls waded in summer, skated in winter, and where May might have told her sister of her dream of touring the Louvre and seeing the bookstalls of Paris reflected in the Seine. Other artists have painted more magnificent pictures than May Alcott did, but the courage to follow her own course, which others belittled, is a story worth passing along. Standing with a friend who says, "Her life matters," I think of the novel I put in a drawer years before with other set-aside manuscripts. I hear a ringing like the bells that were once hung over gravesites, attached to strings in caskets so that those who were thought dead, but weren't, could alert the living and get another chance.

Back Shelves

Summer trips to Maine featured lupine, followed by daisies and day lilies. Now Peter and I see goldenrod and purple asters as we drive up for the weekend. We stop at a used bookstore where my happiest find is a collection of letters written by Ellen Emerson, the daughter of the philosopher, Ralph Waldo Emerson. More to my purposes, Ellen was a friend of May Alcott, another person we know about mostly because she was the relative of someone whose fame lasted beyond death. I bought the two volumes to add to other books from the middle 1800s, such as a volume about herbs to learn what might have been in a garden May weeded, and *The Frugal Housewife,* which helped me to know more about pies, pickles, and the particular ways May and her sisters probably cleaned their homes.

I crack open the first volume while Peter drives, then again in the evening after we walked on the beach and visited friends. As the weekend passed and I skimmed, slogged, and eventually grumbled, Peter reminded me of my initial elation. Fourteen hundred pages can hold a lot of tea parties in which not much happens. I was reading about a period in which both Henry David Thoreau and Nathaniel Hawthorne had died, and I'm pretty sure Mr. Emerson's daughter would have attended those funerals, but nothing is said about them. Their neighbor, Louisa May Alcott, wrote *Little Women,* which proved immediately popular and has never gone out of print, but the novel isn't mentioned.

It's all right. People change their minds about what can or should be forgotten, and what we think of as important may not have seemed so to someone writing at the time. Fortunately, when historians uncover, rescue, and sort, they often preserve the kind of ordinary things that may be found within letters. From Ellen Emerson's correspondence, I learned about the fabrics and cuts of dresses and the varieties of pears in the family's small orchard. May Alcott showing off a spider she painted on her bedroom wall could be worth the twenty-five dollars I paid for these two volumes, along with Ellen's gifts to her when May went abroad for the first time: four bottles of champagne, a hanging pin cushion to nail to her berth, and a copy of *Portraits de Femmes*. She advised May to bring a shawl-strap for her blanket, a basket of oranges, and napkins (handkerchiefs wouldn't be large enough) to spread over her chest when lying on her back in the berth to eat broth or porridge.

I learned that Mrs. Emerson had a habit of screaming if she stubbed her toe or pinched a finger, then might call out an assurance that no bones were broken, then shriek again. I'd have enjoyed some more screams through the dense pages, but I did develop a sense of Concord, Massachusetts about 150 years ago. Catbirds, blue jays, song sparrows, wood pigeons, and red-shouldered blackbirds showed up in the month of May. After a series of burglaries in 1868, Mr. Emerson was reluctant to stray far from the silver cream pitcher.

I browsed, keeping an eye out for mementos small enough to hold or hide in a hand. What people save in pockets, bottom drawers, and bedside tables can carry a story from an ordinary childhood to a remarkable career. Ordinary things may suggest what was important to someone and serve as points on a map of her character. Details about rooms, yards, and cities can suggest ways that my characters might feel connected or distant from their environment, and add tension.

I work my way back as I might with my own memories. So much has faded or frayed, but sometimes catching a scent or a corner of an old calendar will uncover still more. Anyone who has picked up a smooth stone, a ticket stub, a tiny iron from a Monopoly game, even a shoelace or old nickel from a bureau and paused to wonder why it was saved knows there's a lot more to history than what we find in textbooks. We may say *I remember* with a swagger, but if we're truthful, much of what we claim is faint or broken. Which is all right. We can find a lot even on dim paths.

Not every mystery will be solved, but wondering may connect us as much as answers. I spend time with common words that stir the senses the way I once turned over old greeting cards, cotton handkerchiefs, tangled necklaces, and orphaned earrings in my mother's top bureau drawer, looking for clues about who she was. Now that Emily is grown and lives across the country, I similarly wonder as I straighten books, clothing, colored pencils, and photographs she left behind. What will my daughter find in my words and bureau drawers one day? What will connect and what push us apart?

The Sometimes Beautiful Blank Page

No one on my road, neighbors who generally notice just which dog or dogs is with me, would notice anything unusual. No one peeking into my writing room, where I'm spending the cooler days, would see a change either. My handwriting is as messy as ever. Old library books still scent my table.

But I'm changing my focus from poems to prose, trying once again to show May Alcott's life in a historical novel. I'm staying away from my old draft, starting sentences from scratch, wondering: What else? What now? And then? I've often revised manuscripts by letting them sit, then hauling them out, hunkering over, and tackling problems. This time, I'm letting my old draft stay sequestered, relying on my memory and a clean notebook.

Revising by way of the blank page means I don't get the pleasure of seeing pages fill quickly, though every few or fifteen minutes, I haul in a line or two from clear air. But perfectly white paper can make me feel eager, younger, lighter, without piles of old notes to kick aside and assess. Blank paper lets the bossy author fade as I dream my way deeper into my main character, focusing on what I want to show about her life, regardless of the historical context. I keep away from the early drafts so I'm less tempted to follow the old lines and just patch things up. I need to make maps with mistakes and detours in order to find new directions. Knowing much of what happened, this time through I draft new dialogue and scenes, deciding what's most important to the story's arc. I compose new conversations, never mind that I'll have to rake though them later. In this rough draft, I leave repetitions, inconsistencies, and holes, by which I mean visible gaps between sentences, and sometimes, I'm embarrassed to say, within sentences, too.

Sometimes we have to be the well rather than just worry about filling it. Working without looking at old pages gives me new ideas for the flow of events, but also stirs up panic, which I'm trying to ride out with deep breaths, forcing my bottom to stay still. The aloe is leaning over under the weight of its thick, prickly self, waiting to be repotted. Sorry. Even the thirsty geraniums must wait while I stumble through false starts, dead ends, ideas not quite interesting enough.

As the boss of my writing, I set rules, but my managerial style is lenient, so I also offer loopholes. Maybe I'll push my way through a chapter, then open an old folder and help myself to the small gifts of labored-over sentences, paragraphs, maybe occasional whole pages which I can splice in. We'll see. Sometimes just telling myself "You may" is enough to keep me from taking a peek.

My goal is to spend some days close to May's feelings and free will. Time will tell what I get, so time is what I'm trying to give the process. Saying no to the new yarn, the ever-so-attractive unread books, and the spade. I'm trying to be as quiet as the sprawling aloe and paper. The blank page is scary, but with a little work, it isn't blank anymore. Eventually a small voice whispers: *Something is here.* Slowly, a wall starts to look like a window. We can't race to meaning.

Writing sometimes seems like one big game of "Mother, May I?" *Mother, May I take one giant step forward?*

No, but you may take two side steps and three twirls back.

We think we're getting somewhere when … whoops. Writing reminds me of the struggle to move forward to cross a line, but getting the book right matters more than page count. And that just takes time. And the willingness to fall and get up again and keep true to the story that needs to be told.

Plot School on the Porch

We've been gifted with a warm fall, so I'm running a plot school for myself on the porch, trying to put into practice what I know about withholding information, or at least not overwriting, and building on character change. This is what things look like, starting from, ahem, about eight years ago.

1. Write a novel based on a real person, drafting it into what I think is perfection.

2. Hear, more than once, that the characters and situations are interesting, but it's too baggy, full of too much this and that. A historical novelist can get tripped up by fascinating, at least to us, tidbits thrown in that send readers scuttling in too many directions.

3. Put away the manuscript and let the criticism steep. If you're playing along at home, note that the waiting doesn't have to be as extended as it was for me. Just long enough to forget old habits or affection for scenes that took some sweat. I waited while tending to other work, but found that while other manuscripts stayed quiet in their drawer, this one kept up a whisper to come out.

4. Write a rough draft of key scenes without rereading the original draft. This was as difficult as living with a wrapped present from someone whose good taste I could count on. It helped knowing that I could eventually help myself to dialogue and details.

5. Here in Plot School, as I compose and assess scenes, I'm asking myself over and over, How does this incident or conversation make my protagonist see more or less, turn angry or gleeful or morose? When I don't have good answers, I leave some history to history. Readers want to feel invested in a character, a sense that we're building up to revelations. Someone wants something. Someone or something gets in her way. Someone is learning from this.

6. Once or twice a day, I sweep through pages studded with arrows, cross-outs, and letters to indicate where a

paragraph should match up with another. My head is cluttered, too, but without the arrows and alphabet to organize. If I could fit my plot points onto index cards I would, but I think of the scenes as having visible borders and corners where characters can stub their toes. These walls may look low to a more plot-driven writer, but they look high to me. I remember bits of scenes, carefully researched and phrased, that went into the original, but unless I see my character running into them and coming out changed, I'm telling myself to forgo.

7. I'm working as briskly as I can. I have a high tolerance for meandering, which serves me well in research, but there are times when busy readers want to move from A to not just B or C, but Q. And times to let action shift toward theme. Every action of an attentive person has strands that can build tension, for how often do we act with conviction that we're doing something perfectly right? A character's reflections can pull in readers who add their own responses to the braiding between events and a character's sense of whether her choices are right or wrong, apt to lead to trouble or happiness.

8. How's it going? I really don't know. I've had talks to myself about plot before and swore I was listening.

The Sometimes-Soft Bones of a Book

Rain beats down on bare branches. Most red and yellow leaves have fallen, and it's too early to put up the bird feeders: We wait until we're confident that bears are hibernating. During the month between pumpkins on porches and lights strung from bushes, after weeks of composing new pages, I set aside a pile of new pages and let myself crack open the old manuscript. Plundering good lines or scenes, I felt like a giddy pirate, my reward for staying away until the new work was done. Now I'm trying to be choosy as I salvage details and dialogue, using only what will keep to the course I've set.

As I sling old scenes or chapters out the window or fit them into new places, I'm aware of how changing one part makes another wiggle, and must be lopped off. Working with a keener sense of where turns are coming, I can plant signs. When the whole shape or shapelessness of the book feels too much, I go back to concentrate on one small part. It's coming along, like a great serpent flopping and squirming with bones so small you wouldn't guess it had them.

But I remind myself that they're there. Focusing on plot, I keep in mind the power of contrast. For instance, if a relationship begins with some reservation or balking, later flirtations may be more intriguing. At the ends of chapters, should I swerve, say, from tenderness to anger, or from questioning to confidence? A story that seems to have little to do with the theme keeps coming back. This story, small enough to fit in a few lines, has tagged along through a few drafts, though I keep swatting it back to my drawer of cast-offs. If I use this little story it's got to mean something. I can't slip it in just because I think it's cool. It must shift the action to a new direction.

What happens is crucial, but how we react to an event shapes us as individuals, making us grow: the change we look for in a novel. What does the main character need to understand by the end? In *Aspects of a Novel*, E.M. Forster describes narrative as events arranged in sequence, meant to make readers want to know what happens next. He tells us that a novel has a clock, but that time shows not only what we can count, but also value. His example, "I only saw her for five minutes, but it was worth it," has both elements, which a story needs to make us deeply care. We may remember books with scenes we thought took up perhaps a quarter of the book, then reread and find that the scene was just three sentences. They were the three right sentences in the right place, asking readers to put themselves in, and they did.

Just when everything starts to look in order, the plot swells, then flattens. The other evening, I groaned over my laptop and muttered, "Is this book any good?"

Peter looked up from a magazine he was reading at the other end of the table. He said, "I know it will be good. The only question is if it will be good enough for you."

History and Imagination

I'm writing about a real person, but I chose to show her life in a novel rather than nonfiction because while there's plenty of material about May Alcott, who lived in a place and town where lots of people kept diaries and wrote letters, much of what remains leaves out dialogue and thinking that I believe would show her humor, anger, and joy. I pay close attention to what May wrote about herself and what others wrote about her. *Who was she?* twists into questions like *What if?* or *What will happen next? What were her most embarrassing mistakes, and how did she turn them around?*

Taking on the persona of another takes a peculiar humility, or an ability to let myself fade as I enter the world of someone whose life is different from mine. I listen as I would to someone I hope will become a sort of friend, noting what's said and looking for what might link us. I also need *chutzpah*. While the humble writer keeps quiet in the corners, another part of me must stalk in wearing big boots. I have a sense of importance that shouldn't run over into entitlement. I think I can get most things right, and brim with eagerness to try.

Our lives are full of both not knowing and knowing, modesty and arrogance, and writing is like that, too. It feels great to think we've got a grip, but more often we're at least a little lost. It's okay. We may have to wander off track to appreciate the path we finally make. We like the assertive smack of landing on ground, but need the wobble of lifting, the temporary imbalance. When we meet people, we juggle all we hear and see, sizing up a tone, the way she holds her arms, looks or doesn't look at others, then we use the inexact art of guessing to get to know them.

A writer of historical fiction, too, decides to live with what seem the best, if not definitive, answers. Knowing we might be wrong is as crucial as thinking that we're right. And truly understanding someone? Comprehension can't be graded as true or false, any more than the lines between nonfiction and fiction are as clear as library classifications might make them seem.

We try to inch ahead, and history reels us back. The past doesn't stand still as a monument, but flickers like shadows and light. Much as I like fading wallpaper or mud brick walls, ladder-back chairs or stone benches, what I write is really about how nothing changes much. Over the years and centuries, people are much like you and me, carrying the promise of return, continuity, and everything having its season. Bringing me back to my shiny silver laptop on an old wooden desk.

Ready! Set! Now Sit Very Still

I don't recommend becoming a writer to those who can't tolerate a life of little drama. Back when Emily was in first grade, her teacher told me she was surprised to learn that she dreamed of a career as a waitress, but it didn't surprise me. I could imagine that ferrying ice cream sundaes topped with gummy bears looked more fun than sitting still in front of a computer.

I'm afraid it's not all fireworks all the time at my desk. When I'm tempted to abandon my novel, it helps to remember other people who had it much harder. I may call up the great role models of obsession, such as Marie Curie, who stirred scrapings from forest floors for four years, hoping she'd isolate a new element. Or Mary Anning, who day after day, month after month, chiseled stone to reveal fossils, chipping in increasingly smaller increments. Both scientists showed a high tolerance for process over result. Marie Curie had to be satisfied with the dream of what she'd name radium, Mary Anning with the sense that the world was older than her neighbors thought. Really, writers are lucky. We get to marvel at the way we can twist a sentence and find something fresh.

Still, I'm not immune to boredom, and have learned a few tricks to keep from sinking there. When one section of a book gets tiresome, I often switch to another scene. When I tell my procrastinating self that she's getting a break, luckily she hardly notices. I've given her another task. Sometimes I deliberately work on a chapter ahead, then, wanting the one before to look just as pretty, head back. Stepping away from what held my conscious attention lets my unconscious kick in. Once I tell myself that my work is done, a pretty new phrase may show up or I'll spot a new way for a chapter to turn.

A big book can be overwhelming, which is a cousin to boredom, so I divide up the pages, employing corkboards or pink and green paper clips to finesse manageable blocks.

In a pinch, I can line up those paper clips, or turn them into star shapes. Is my restlessness something I have to stick out or a sign to shake things up? I think we have to get down a string of words while ignoring a desire to brew more tea, weed the garden, or hang out with the dogs. There's that hammock, and always another book to read. We've got to shut out the siren voices and work, but without forgetting the spirit of play that reminds us to take chances. Maybe we do want to risk changing points of view, or let characters who didn't speak to each other before sit side by side, or brawl, or kiss. We can look under what we made of words, check the basement, and then look up, too. Maybe there are fireworks after all.

Cards We Carry

This is the first time I've been in the classroom Pat shares with a remedial math teacher, who has taken on the additional role of reminding Pat when she's due for her meds. About ten years ago, Pat switched from teaching Special Ed to teaching reading to children who are learning English as a second language. Under hand-colored paper flags of the many nations these third, fourth, and fifth graders left behind, Pat has displayed some of my books. Not all, not just because some would be too difficult for them, but because she thinks at least one is too sad. I remember back when Pat and I both taught high school. My colleagues in the English Department were cynical men who smelled of cigarettes, while the Special Ed teachers tended to wear pastel and send around notes with happy faces. I was somewhere in between. I got annoyed when Pat asked me for vocab lists for *To Kill a Mockingbird*, and when I insisted that I'd rather students understood how it might feel to be Scout or Boo Radley than get the spelling right, she got annoyed that I couldn't seem to understand that her students needed practical, literal directions. We found common ground, but over all our years of friendship, she's still someone who believes in resolute cheer. As a writer, I want to show things in all their nuance, complication, and sometimes darkness. I try to watch with a steady eye, not rush toward feel-good twists or silver linings.

Pat had told me that the students in her current class had not only left their first homes, but some had parents who fought brutally, or had died of drug overdoses, or were in prison. Some of these students might choose to see pain and fears like their own reflected in books, but Pat's way is to offer a haven in this room. This means that she's been vague with the students about her absences from work, and tries to cover up signs of her cancer and its treatment. I feel uneasy with this evasion, but her principal, who'd said, "Absolutely, yes," to another teacher with cancer who'd asked to bring a nurse and counselor into her classroom to answer questions, has respectfully left how Pat deals with her illness to Pat.

Maybe I am more like those disgruntled English teachers than I thought. I tell myself not to be so critical, but can't work myself up to the cheers that some of Pat's friends manage, calling her a warrior. I'd never thought of Pat in military or mythic terms, and don't see why I should change now. Yes, it's better to look on the bright side than its opposite, but there's light that comes and goes no matter what we wish, and is not connected to on and off switches. There's beauty in shadows that shift like feelings, or even the folded card with a picture of a sand dollar that Pat has kept in her wallet long enough so the creases have broken. She recently showed me this get well card I'd sent her decades ago, and while I recognized my old handwriting, I didn't ask to read it. It's her artifact now, her history.

Pat introduced me to her students as an author, pointing to the books on her shelf. I'm sure she'd explained to them that I wrote the words inside, but no one's face opened as if they grasped the concept of a real person behind words in print. Writing books seemed distant to children who were still struggling to learn to read. What most of them wanted, and needed, was an audience for their growing skills. Pat and I passed around books, giving them chances to read to us. We praised them for reaching the ends of sentences.

Then we celebrated with ice cream. Pat was embarrassed that a guest should dish out refreshments, but it was clear the metal scoop was difficult to hold in her hands made raw from the chemo. I asked one of the oldest and quietest girls to pass around the bowls. Pat said that this girl is thinking of becoming a writer, and I realize she's the one that Pat had confided earlier came from a home that was not what a home should be. Without going into detail, she said that her good reading scores placed her out of this classroom, but it was decided that she and her sister would be best off sticking together, leaving for middle school at the same time. This is a school where the safety of two girls comes before test results.

After cleaning up, I asked this girl to help me carry my bags back to my car, though I'd lugged them in with no trouble. I sensed she liked standing beside me. Classes began to be dismissed, and we stopped in the hallway. As one group of students left their classroom to head for the busses, their teacher joined the other adults by the corridor walls. The principal left her office, ladies left the cafeteria, and the custodians came out to smile and wave, as if this were a parade. Wherever these children were going, they had this moment of being watched with care.

I smiled and waved, too. In one of my bags was a pretty journal given to me that I won't use because my handwriting and habits are such that I do most of my writing on my laptop. I worried that it was too small a gift, but I handed it to the girl I hoped would keep writing.

Then I left with Pat, thinking again about the card with the picture of a sand dollar in her wallet. Too soon, someone will empty that wallet, and perhaps keep nothing but bills and change. But for now she carries the card, quiet as the confidences she gets from students, as the whispers and quick hugs she gives back.

Pauses

For about twenty minutes last week, I thought the first chunk -- just over half of my novel -- was ready to send to my writing group for comments. I felt the triumph of finishing for at least the length of time it takes to down a first-of-the-season pumpkin ale. I didn't make giddy announcements, just a quiet, "Done," with a wiggle in the word, like a question mark, to Peter, who was absorbed in his own thoughts at the kitchen table.

You might think I know better than to make even a quiet pronouncement, and I do. I just wanted to keep that ta-da feeling a bit longer. But after I excised some dialogue and polished some descriptions, the first section of the novel I'm calling *Little Woman in Blue* didn't look so very done. The prose was woven, but I still found places to poke in a pencil. Dealing with ragged edges left at the ends of sentences and scenes, the process that I began calling editing is looking more like writing.

It's okay. If I try to mend too early, I'll miss making the cracks that might let me and my readers enter more deeply. I think of the characters in my work as important friends, who need me a little longer. I know them pretty well, but maybe I should consider them in a few new places, let them wander, nap, continue or cut short a conversation. It's great when characters surprise us, just like the real people we assume we know. I need to let my characters change their clothes, let prose I once thought was shiny crumble, then shape it up again.

As I chop out pages and paragraphs, the spaces left remind me of how some impressionists kept white spaces between paint strokes to show a sense of movement and keep the surface alive. So even during these final-ish stages, I don't send away my muse, or unconscious, or capricious part of my mind. I want to keep the feeling I have before opening a trunk in an attic, before I'm amazed or disappointed. Instead of hunkering over the computer, I sit back and mull, prod images to see if they'll crack open. I need to roughhouse some sentences into place, but also to put up my feet and see what words float by, to balance effort and letting go. The table is set, but with spaces left to move silverware or soup bowls.

Making Friends with the Secretary in the House

The stack for the first half or two thirds gets thicker. I just broke past three hundred finished pages, which is long for the midpoint, even for a historical novel. I don't think I'm being profligate with words, on the rebound from writing poetry, though I like allowing conversations to meander and build to grand misunderstandings or fleeting moments of love. Themes include those of sisterhood, art, and romance, which take space, and at this point while keeping an eye for sprawl, I'm allowing in words I'm bound to take out, leaving my bigger shears for later. My manuscript is starting to look both book-like and over-familiar. This is when I know I need fresh eyes, beginning with those of my writing group. I count on them to revive my energy for the project, so I'll feel up to looping long and short threads, yanking out stray threads, and tearing new gaps that will need stitching.

I'm working quickly because I promised to have something for our meeting. I love a deadline, especially one that's harrowing mostly in my mind: my friends wouldn't sneer or even complain if I asked for a few more weeks. But after a lot of moving between pages, it's time to stand firmly in one place for the two weeks the members of my group will take to read it. This draft is fun because I want it to be as good as I can make it, and because I'll get another chance for fixing before I send it to the city. There's a sense of forgiveness around my fingers. It's like cleaning the house for an easy guest: say my sister, who grew up with our mother's strong tolerance for clutter. I want clear places to sit and prefer piles that don't teeter, but I don't yet have to worry about dust on high shelves or whatever lurks under the beds.

Still, I must leave dreamy if dedicated mulling and face pages riddled with cross-outs and notes I posted to myself, like "Make stronger!" or "Too smarmy?" I work until the gaps between good sentences get smaller. Words topple into place – click, clack, click. The characters are speaking up. Scenes find their right places in chapters. Even the arc is starting to look sturdy. I check for carelessness with nature, aiming to be a stickler on knowing which sorts of birches like full light and which willows need damp ground. It's good to pay attention to the varieties of plants and animals. A robin that flies too high or a plant that blooms in the wrong season can take readers out of the dream we want our stories to seem.

Now I seem so close to a final draft that I have the fantasy that all I need is a good typist to pull together my notes. But it seems the narrow-eyed typist I call in has different ideas. She hardly types a sentence, before muttering: *No way will you get away with that.*

Did I request a secretary with an opinion? No. I want to shove her from the room. Except that she's me. And she's got her points. I find scenes to add and others to fatten up. Does something important happen on every page? I compress time that I'd expanded before. I let conversations go on a bit longer, though this means rambling happens, which I have to cut. I ask if every character is both clear and complicated. Is every "she said" needed? Can I change some names to pronouns, or should some pronouns be names? I try switching the order of clauses to see if a picture might come more forcefully to a reader's mind. I reshape dialogue so that one person is actually talking to another – not, as in the earlier draft, one person going on too long, talking to herself, or one person supplying both halves of the conversation. I read aloud, listening for a rhythm, seeing if sentences fall without having to gasp for breath.

As I revise, I don't let the poet-in-me entirely disappear. She stays alert for alliteration, and blots most out. She's attentive to cadence, and makes sure it seems honest. She hunkers over images with hands open like a child eager to catch a cricket. And as a novelist-at-the-moment, I get to follow with a wildly waving net.

Such work is subjective and tricky, especially as judgments are made by someone who's at least a little worn out and restless. But at last the opinionated typist gives me a curt nod of approval. We call the piece perfect enough for now. Writing means making mistakes, fixing some, forgiving myself for others (which isn't the same as being complacent), and moving on. I send my pages to my critique group and open my notes on the novel's second half.

Mini Lesson in Writing a Picture Book

When people ask me how I came to write for young people in particular, I tell them how I began after Peter and I had a child, and in the natural course of events, read and reread books by Margaret Wise Brown, Eric Carle, and Dr. Seuss. Perhaps like many a sleep-deprived parent, I thought: I could write this stuff. I also knew that smooth sentences can trick readers into thinking they were oh-so-smooth to write.

After years of writing, some of my picture books were published. Now I teach graduate students who are getting degrees in writing for children, which means I get to reread picture books and consider how they were constructed. I ask my students to closely observe the text, illustration, design, and how these interrelate, before they write their own manuscripts. While I like longer picture books and protest the way that once children learn to read, they're often swiftly directed away from illustrations, the classic picture book is for people who still regularly sit on laps or attend story times. Short books tend to sell most these days, and so while students will go on to write in styles and lengths that best suit them, in class I'll challenge them to keep a text between the word count of *Good Night, Moon* (146) and *Where the Wild Things Are* (338). We spend a lot of time in class considering springy and shapely narratives, but when asked, as I recently was on the phone, how to write a picture book, I refrained from pointing out that I studied English in college and grad school, continued reading lots of books, wrote a zillion pages that never worked out, regularly bang my head on my desk, and keep myself still until something pretty appears on paper.

Instead I said, "Watch the balance of what's a lesson and what's fun. Most books have something to teach, but you want to stay in the child character's view as much as you can. Or you can make that child an animal or creature, more apt to have adventures without a parent to worry about them. Keep words and sentences fairly simple. You don't want to go on and on. Most picture books are thirty-two pages when printed, so while your manuscript can be written without indicating page breaks, some writers make what's called a book dummy. Take eight sheets of paper and divide them by four, then make sure you have short, perfect material for each of those pages, (saving a few for front matter, such as copyright notes, and end pages). You want action. Avoid talking heads. It can't hurt to include a dog."

If I get another call, I might add that it's good to take a long look at some of the greats, like *Make Way for Ducklings, Corduroy, Roxaboxen,* or *The Lorax,* and also more current award-winners. Picture books are like poems not only in that they're often designed to be read aloud and that the best evoke something grand with just a few words, but, sadly, in that too many people think they can write them without steeping themselves in the genre. I remember the first time I went to the children's department of the library without a toddler's hand in mine. I felt sneaky as I approached the desk with a small armful of books, but left with a just-hit-up-the-candy-store feeling, part guilt, more elation.

Once home, I read through my stack of books about shoes, suppers, snow, sisters, balls, balloons, brothers, dinosaurs, and the drama of going to bed. Picture books ultimately must be read aloud, but I found the words rang differently in my head in a room with no plastic animals on the floor. Not distracted by interruptions or thoughts of when I might turn off the lamp, I enjoyed the way a story began with immediacy, curved gorgeously, and ended with a happy thump or hum. Sometimes it begged me to go back around again.

Writers should find subjects that truly move us. Some have a bent for the fantastical, while others can't fake an interest in dragons and charmed castles. Some people are naturally amusing, while others of us have to decide how much bleakness will add to a sense of truth and how much children should be sheltered. Sadness doesn't surprise most children. Peter Rabbit's father was eaten in a pie. *Goodnight, Moon* may or may not have a subtext of death, but isn't that what so many children fear when the lights are turned off?

There's hardly a fairy tale without wolves, swords, spells, poison, or someone getting lost in a forest. Children may find consolation in stories and sanctuaries that include spaces behind sofas, attics, basements, tents, tree houses, gardens, or fire escapes, any place with dark corners or alcoves that have both a sense of safety and traces of fear that foster imagination.

We grownups may have differences in vocabulary, height, and hairstyles from children, and there are often gaps in the amount of time we want to spend watching bulldozers or even the cat, but we may find the same things amusing or amazing. A writer of picture books is writing for children first and foremost, but it's all right to please her own tastes, too, as long as they're ones that accept people as they are, and not wanting to nudge them into being someone else. We want to keep children rapt and perhaps prod them into more civilized behavior, staying aware of both our possibly squirmy audience and those who buy them books. Picture books offer brevity, brilliance, and often humor. What's not to like?

Outside, Looking In

Teaching Children's Literature means I get to reread books with a very deep rabbit hole, a yellow brick road, the Hundred Acre Wood, and Never-never Land. My students are mostly college seniors and English majors, who not coincidently were introduced to books by parents who read aloud. Many like both returning to old favorites or reading books they missed as children, sometimes because they hadn't yet been written, or because they seemed old fashioned, or because TV or movie versions served as substitutes. Often there's delight in finding levels of *Winnie-the-Pooh* missed when their concerns were more about honey jars and wayward balloons. *Corduroy,* a stuffed bear who lost a button and perhaps a chance at love, makes a quest through a department store at night, as terrifying in its way as any epic. The artistry of *Where the Wild Things Are* is sometimes more appreciated through the years.

There are also disappointments, such as finding the prose of *The Wizard of Oz* flat, or fretting about how they'd missed stereotypes or injustices in this or that novel. None of this means they shouldn't have loved what they loved. The story of Dorothy and her friends in Oz is amazing enough not to call for creative syntax. And some students may choose to read to their children as some of their parents did, gently pointing out narrow or misguided views within a work even while they savor other parts. Like every other class in the English Department, Children's Literature is ridden with reminders of how easy it is to find flaws. We tear apart books, trying to figure out how they work, and point to awkward sentences, clichés, laughable coincidences, and plot holes. At some point in class somebody protests. "But I love this book!"

Yes, many of us do. We nod, then go back to analysis, while the writer in me remembers gorgeous carpets made with one intentional flaw as a reminder of beautifully imperfect human hands. Is there any work of art that's without rough patches?

A student just told me about writing a critical paper while under-her-breath begging the author for forgiveness. We can pick apart the prose, then go back and cherish some words the way we'd accept any gift: perhaps not looking so closely, but simply treasuring the exchange. Many of us hold imperfect books dear. So what do we call this in a classroom? Maybe what it's called outside: Wonder. There are moments when we stop reading or talking and adore a page. In literature as in life, sometimes what seems random, sloppy, vague, or even wrong is more inviting than a smooth surface or clear message.

As a professor, I encourage dismantling sentences or books to understand how they might have been made, but as a creator, I don't set theme, structure, and tone on the table as a shoemaker might line up measuring tools, knives, and leather, ready to clip or stitch away. It's a messy process. I've been asked if writers are better off innocently putting together what others might take apart, or should we study literary theory?

I choose some of both. I begin writing when snagged by a person or image I follow, but at some point I start to identify structures. Then, what Aristotle, Joseph Campbell, or other how-to-and-why sorts wrote about exposition, rising action, or resolution can suggest a frame. We all work within traditions. I've never set out with the idea that a stanza or paragraph needs a simile or metaphor, but while I'm poking an image to check what's inside, I might realize a metaphor flickers under my pen. If I lift the point at the right time, I can set it loose. Perhaps this would happen if I hadn't studied figures of speech, but my guess is not so much. This may be why many of us collect books on craft. Something happens in that gap between thinking about our work specifically and considering it in general terms.

Studying the work of literary critics may make some writers feel self-conscious. Anything that stalls us for long is probably good to avoid. But I find it's useful to refer to the experts during some of the many rounds of revision. Sometimes when I'm on my window seat wearing a turtleneck pulled over my chin, sweatpants, and fingerless gloves, I can call in the better-dressed person who draws narrative arcs on the chalkboard or quotes Coleridge.

What's gleaned from scholars can give me enough of a shake to see what's under my hands with revived attention. So I return to writing without keeping my eye on a plan, perhaps maneuver a few strings and wires, then come out for another look at the whole.

One Hundred Pages

Maybe this has happened to you: You're happily moving forward through the second half of your revision, thinking you've finally got the hang of writing novels. Maybe you can see where this story is going and are empathetically stiffening your shoulders the way I did while listening to someone in my writing group go through the requisite but always too short list of things I did right in the first 270 pages. Then she calmly said that about one hundred pages need to go. And I still need to find a plot.

My two other friends nodded. I nodded, too, trying to hide my gritted teeth. As I eventually packed up three copies of these 270 pages, which I'd given them to mark up, I tried not to look like someone who'd been gently told she didn't get something she'd been trying long and hard to get. I didn't sleep well.

In the morning, I remind myself that if all three people in my writing group think something, they're usually right. I start making my way through their notes and my manuscript, ripping out a sentence here, a paragraph or page there. I'm buoyed by the occasional "nice" in some margins. It's not all bad! But a little historical detail can go far, with too much distracting from the line I mean to propel or at least nudge a reader onward. I delete scenes that round out characters, but don't either block or pave a way to forward movement. I take out the pink and sky blue index cards, and at some point I'll actually use them. *What does she want? What's stopping her?* I murmur.

As I twist a blade over pages I'm no longer numbering but calling a bunch, I work more quickly than my usual meandering -- a word I prefer to sluggish -- pace. Being one of the world's slowest writers has its good points, but there's something to be said for going against my instincts from time to time. Changing the setting on my speed dial can sweep me to new places. Shaking off my attachment to what's there may give me a better grip on what can be. Not haste but a steady clip may make me bump into things and forge connections. Momentum can push me over distractions, though like papers written the night before they're due, this may work better in beautiful youth. At any rate, it's like ripping off a bandage. Why prolong the pain as I cross out words on the way to what most matters? So I'm kicking it up a notch. There come times when every tortoise should put on bunny ears and hustle.

When I worry that I'm letting too much go, I console myself that those sentences, paragraphs, chapters have not vanished forever. They're just stored, like clothes I know won't fit again, but can't quite give away. The computer's cut-and-paste means that nothing that's done today can't be undone tomorrow. So I start a new file called "Lovely Discards," and whip past caution. I drink coffee, not herbal tea, play Springsteen, not Vivaldi, as I not only flash my scissors, but look for ways to punch up what is left. Some scenes aren't necessarily out of place, but distant, and I try to amp up the heartbeat. I heighten action and trim down the beauty-for-its-own sake. I've got to raise the volume, make sure the reasons for each chapter are more apparent.

I think of how some artists begin with gesture drawings: a model may pose for half a minute, sometimes two, while artists sketch with charcoal or soft pencil to catch a sense of motion. They begin in a rush, timer clicking, then later work out a likeness. At some point they may go back to the original energy, trying not to entirely cover their tracks with information about surfaces and shadows. Now I'm making, or looking for, the lines that convey speed or at least motion. We should know when to creep and when to dash, when we're properly setting things in order and when it's time to stop, careful not to rub out signs of the initial, energetic inspiration and uncertainty.

My vision is getting clearer, even if my timetable got a little longer. Now that I've stopped wincing, I can appreciate my friend's advice "to whittle away the slower, more repetitive scenes so that the magnificent scenes can really shine." I check to see that each scene develops the complexity of the characters, moves the plot forward, deepens the theme, or all of the above. Can I combine some characters, scenes, or subplots? I check the beginnings and ends of the book, chapters, scenes, and paragraphs for lines of explanation and over-explanation to cut. These can add up. I make new transitions, some swifter than before. Sometimes a simple line break or a single sentence is the best way to shift though time and space. We can write, "The next day," or "A month passed," which, being almost invisible, is often better than transitional scenes.

Cutting part of my manuscript by about a third seemed impossible, but it turns out it wasn't. There's more muscle to my work now, less sag. Finally my shoulders drop back where they belong. I remember the tough love of a good critique group, which is just the kind of love I need, even if I whimpered, and I apologize for that. Criticism of one's writing isn't about a self, or soul, and it shouldn't be about ego. It's about getting what's in one head into another's. It's about loving the characters and getting their stories told.

Researching and Revising the Past

I wasn't trained as a historian or journalist, so my fact-finding skills were learned along the way and often hinge on whim and intuition. Solitary researching suits my temperament more than interviewing, though both can be necessary for historical novelists and have a lot in common. Researchers don't know just which book or archive may provide what detail we'll need, and journalists don't know which conversation will be fruitful. Many reporters point out the crucial role of listening, learning when to stop asking questions to leave room for answers. They assess versions of so-called truth told by different people. They may note not only what someone is saying, but what they're not. They stay alert for contradictions between words and gestures, a clash between how someone wants to be seen and how they are.

Historical novelists do this, too, though our conversations may be with the dead. We have to teach a bit, but not look like we're expounding. We want to show another time, but shared themes or feelings should pulse underneath. I try to hedge what historian Jill Lepore identifies as two ways that history can split from truth: One is that people in the past were simpler or kinder. The other is that people get better as time progresses. We want past settings that shed light on present day issues, but watch the ways that the present colors our view of the past. It's a balancing act to keep the perspectives of characters true to their times, while still trying to forge connections with contemporary readers.

We generally consider two major audiences. One knows little about the era we're writing about, and we have to set a stage without making the furniture look obviously arranged. Other readers know a lot, and one false or even unnecessary fact may break the sort of spell we want our story to stir. We can find anachronisms in Shakespeare, but he didn't have Google. We do, so it's our job to find out when men wore cravats and how they tied them and the right names for whatever women put on their feet. Even if we can whip out research to prove that something existed, if an early reader questions something like would this woman wear shoes or sandals, we have to decide whether sticking with the surprising reality will bring readers too far out of the story.

Researching history may be richest when we don't stop with known heroes, such as the names of those leading a parade to celebrate the end of the Civil War, but try to find views such as a child crammed between hoop skirts might see. I aim for enough detail to give readers a sense that I know what I'm talking about, books that summon with a sense of time and place, but aren't weighed down by it. We want more than characters wearing historically right clothes, sitting on period furniture. Facts should be woven into the narrative so readers don't spot the author as researcher trying to smuggle in cherished findings. We try to trim until the research doesn't call attention to itself, like a badge. We may need to show just one glimpse into a shop window, not the name of every store on the street or the names of their proprietors, even if we went to some trouble to learn those. Some places need to fade as they do for most of us as we distractedly wend our way through familiar rooms and streets.

Whether our research ever makes it to the page, and whether it comes from books or from walking where someone else walked, it changes us. Even small things may give us a sense of what someone valued and feared. We have to remember not only what the characters know, but what they don't know. Writing about May Alcott, I keep in mind not only that she didn't know who would return from the battlefields, but who would win the Civil War. I look for words that sound authentic but don't stand out. I reread *Little Women* and other books written during the time when May lived. I lifted a few phrases, such as "it will do him a world of good" and "Christopher Columbus," which I allowed myself just once, along with an occasional "Mercy!" I used the Internet to check some word choices, for along with excellent dictionaries citing word origins, we can find sites devoted to anachronisms. I want language authentic to the period, but when a word jars, jostles, or knocks story even briefly to the side, I look for others.

It's good to read aloud. Does the dialogue sound natural, following rhythms like those heard around us, with the right sorts of insistence or hesitation? Just because people lived in an age where some customs were more formal than ours doesn't mean that their dialog was stilted. I try to make sure that some questions are left unanswered or replied to indirectly, the way people talk in life. But unlike what can be realistic, it's best to keep characters from digressing so far that readers might lose the thread.

After all our vetting, we should come back to what we know as people. Artifacts such as photographs, licenses, or even letters never tell us everything. For instance, while I treasure my wedding albums, there are other memories from the day I value more. We want to get the details right, then return to story.

Rows of Empty Chairs

Last night I walked down a sidewalk to a bookshop, turning at a sign adorned with bright balloons to welcome a debut author, someone I know, but we don't keep up. I was excited that she'd written a book and eager to hear some passages. Then I was embarrassed to be the only person there. She'd done other readings locally, and might have used up her allotment of friends likely to come. When she told me she'd hoped people who didn't know her might attend, I shook my head and said something I meant to be soothing about busy lives. She shook her own head harder, and said, "People suck." I laughed. She laughed. It wasn't kind or entirely true. It wasn't a slogan for a t-shirt I'd choose to wear. But I've felt that sinking feeling in front of rows of empty folding chairs, too. And the words were better than what she said next, voicing her dread that no one came because something in her was unlikeable.

No, no, no, no, no. Unattended or sparsely attended readings, like bad weather, just happen. They're not a consequence of our character flaws.

As we talked, and it became increasingly clear that no one else was coming, she asked me to go get something to eat with her, rather than stand in the shop. The hour allotted for a reading and signing wasn't over, and the booksellers mentioned that someone might still show up, but my friend was pretty sure that waiting was a lost cause. I kind of wish we stayed, or at least helped put away the chairs. Booksellers who were kind enough to host an event should not be left with a memory of an author fleeing. But I was following her lead, like the booksellers who told her, "You can do what you want. This is your event."

She and I walked to a restaurant where I answered some of her authorly questions and coached persistence. We also talked about our families, friends, and other work. As she's someone I hadn't seen in years, there was not only lots to catch up on, but a theme of loss. It's not just published books that don't turn out exactly the way we expected. Almost everything and everyone surprises us.

Life is not a dream, despite what some of us sang as children while pretending to row a boat. We can make plans, but few will blossom as beautifully as we imagined. When our makeshift castles fall flat, we're advised to accept things as they are or look for what's good amidst the rubble. We can cry or curse because only one person came to a reading, or be glad that the two of us got to have a salad and glass of wine. But while keeping an eye out for rainbows, we shouldn't forget to include, "People suck" in the conversation. Disappointment is part of the dinner.

Perhaps always, but probably now more than ever, a writer's work includes doing some publicity, such as making ourselves available for readings, talks, or book fairs. I don't do much soliciting for appearances, but my policy is to generally say yes when asked to do things. At stores and fairs, I try to keep in mind that if one person shows up, she may be an encouraging friend, a cute child, a funny stranger, or a teacher who knows somebody who knows somebody who might buy some books. School visits and conferences are usually rewarding because of built-in audiences, but one never knows their impact. We're likely to inspire some and disappoint others, something I was recently reminded of when telling a friend about a fabulous panel I'd heard, then listening to her relate her waste-of-time experience with another, until I caught a detail and realized that we'd attended the same panel. And sales resulting from such talks are unpredictable. I recently spoke to a packed audience at a hotel, and while few left the ballroom getting out credit cards, when I came to the table with my books, I was greeted by a young hotel guest wearing a bathing suit and with hair fragrant from chlorine. Her mom and grandmother snapped her picture while she happily waved *Get Set! Swim!*

Another time I spoke with several other children's authors, then left the auditorium for the gym where our books were displayed for sale on tables. Long lines formed of people waiting for signatures from well-known authors. One girl and her mom stood before the folding table displaying my books. The mother told me that they were adopting a child from India, and that her daughter had woven a way between the tables, finally returning to *Aani and the Tree Huggers* because the girl on its cover looked a bit like the girl who'd soon become her sister. Amid the hubbub, our eyes meeting each other's made a quiet place.

What could be better? Still, I have to sell books if I want a contract to publish another one. This is an era when many of us know writers who've stopped writing, book sellers who've closed great shops, editors who've left or lost jobs in a field they once loved, librarians with small budgets, and teachers with too many students or tests to teach the ways they believe are best. Writers do what we can to help our books find an audience, but all the balloons in the world might not draw in people, and shouting for attention for a quiet book seems likely to make people cross the street to avoid megaphones meant to lure them in. When do we stop beating the drum or try an entirely new tune?

There aren't easy answers for those of us authors who are marketers by default. But it's good to have a friend or stranger remind us that the short rows of empty chairs aren't who we are. We've done our work, leaving traces of ourselves in our words with all the honesty and clarity we can muster. Then we let them go.

The Day after Thanksgiving

The day after a gathering, full of recollections in tranquility, often feels more gratitude-packed than the busy day. The dishes are all washed, thanks to Pat, who arrived with champagne, cake, and blue plastic gloves, since she insists on helping clean up, which includes rinsing plates before loading them into the dishwasher. Leftovers are stowed away, thanks to our friend, Jess, who dances even when she's just looking for plastic wrap and whirling things into it. The dogs are sated from scraps and extra head scratches, and the cat comes out of hiding. I read and let my mind drift back in thanks for the day with friends and relatives. I'm planning to get back to work on finishing my last chapters, when, what's this calling for my attention? A new idea? For a completely different book?

Muses knock at inconvenient times. It's lovely when thoughtful guests at the door hand me chocolates, which can be shared right away, and I'm always happy for flowers. I'm grateful for a fresh image for my present work. But when the muse pulls up in a battered truck to let me know she's got a new book idea, what does a proper hostess do?

I settle in my chair, listen, and start a new folder, filled with the beckoning voices of the new. There's all that possibility, the salty taste of what's unknown. I hear the promises and don't yet know the problems. Sometimes the muse tosses in ideas for my work-in-progress. I smile politely, and don't mention that I wish the suggestion for a scene arrived when I was actually working on that chapter.

I enjoy an interruption as much as anyone, but at some point in the muse's visit, I'll unplug the teakettle, stack the dishes in the sink, and loudly clear my throat. New ideas may glitter and smell like cotton candy, but I love my old manuscript for better or for worse, in sickness and in health, to swipe a line. There are fewer surprises, but there are still surprises. Only I can give myself the sweet shuffling sound of a manuscript's final pages falling into place.

Winter: Finding an End

When I've told other writers that I finished a manuscript, some mention that they've never had a chance to say that. Their eyes glint with possibility, and maybe a bit of jealousy. But I expect my eyes have only a normal level of shine. Coming to the final sentence of the last chapter is one moment of a long stretch. One final-ish draft goes to my writing group, then comes back for corrections. Then there's the labor of finding an editor, which has taken four months at best for me, six years at worst, not counting manuscripts that remain in drawers. I don't have one of those lovely "she read it on the subway and called me the next morning" stories. Even after the book is in covers and ready for readers who don't know me, I've got to see what I can do to reach those in the business of getting the book into the hands of reviewers, librarians, and other good people who like to read. And it's good to celebrate each step, clinking mugs of tea if not flutes of champagne, especially when the end of one book means another is underway.

Last Chapters

I've been looking forward to this day, but now that I'm finishing up my novel, I'm nostalgic for the beginning, when I made allowances for messes. The end means it's not only time to clean up every evident stray line, and scrape away repetitions and contradictions, but I miss the old sense of hope that comes with first chapters. I have to leave behind the dream and recognize the reality. It can be more fun to dress for a party than to go.

Never mind. I get back to work, trying to be as careful as a jeweler chipping a precious gem, knowing the right angle can let in more light, but a too-hasty tap can make a stone crumble. I'm not only cautious that I don't go overboard and end up where I began --with a blank page -- but I weigh words and even punctuation. I also pay attention to what a good ending needs. A memorable scene, and maybe a surprise that isn't too corny, but risks sentimentality. We want to give readers something to hold while marking how something dear seems to be sliding away. Edith Wharton reminds us that "one should always be able to say of a novel: 'It might have been longer,' never: 'It need not have been so long.'"

A good ending might have the poignance of a wedding toast, combining a look back with a look ahead. Edith Wharton is among the many who note that a novel's ending should be suggested on the first page. I'm playing with images, realizing that I have pine boughs on page one, and can slip in the scent of evergreens on the last page. An ending should have some sense of completion, but not land with the thud of a bad punch line or be as stiff as a slogan stuck at the end of a fable. An ending may flicker like the candles people used to set in windows during storms, a sign so those who wandered or were lost could know that here is a safe haven. Yet such a place would hold mysteries, too. Who exactly would we meet inside?

Putting on Brakes near the End of the Hill

I recently had lunch with a friend who told me she'd taken time off from her novel, after a day she'd spent crying over a manuscript that seemed a waste of the several years she'd devoted to it.

"Aren't you almost done?" I asked.

She nodded. I nodded. Reaching the end of a book can be a dangerous time. Anxiety ratchets up. Typing "the end" means showing it to people. Could the old dream turn into a nightmare? What if everyone hates it? What if they're right?

I don't think this is the time to take a break, but maybe take extra long walks, pet the dog, schedule a massage, or read books you won't be tempted to compare to yours. Finishing means facing the fact that we haven't said everything and having to accept that we won't. We have to believe that what we've managed is good enough, a skill some of us are better at than others. We give up the good company we've had on the page, and fear can pervade this sense of loss. The heart-stopping, breath-holding moment when our finger hits *send* may be followed by un-thrilling silence, too apt to get filled with second guesses about the book's quality. We must brace ourselves for rejections we may choose to call by another name. Perhaps someone will say, "Not quite. Do you care to start again?" and we must decide how we'll answer.

A time comes to pry ourselves away and trust that a new book will come as this one did, or in an entirely different way: from hovering over a blank page, reading, hiking, flossing our teeth, wandering through a museum, or sitting on a bus with our ears and eyes wide open. Just as we can train ourselves to write or at least edit a paragraph in a dentist's office or waiting for a child to finish playing soccer, it's good to fill in the waiting to hear back about a book with another project. I don't mean to sound glib. I fret and fritter time as much as anyone. But I find comfort in making something new. We go forth again, being a hopeful species, including those who scratch lottery tickets, park for just three minutes by a fire hydrant, return to a dentist who hurt us, marry for the third time, buy chocolate peanut butter cups in two packs and tell ourselves we'll eat just one, plant another crop of beans where rabbits ate the last, or set off on a journey without a map, decent directions, GPS, or a friend who can tell north from south.

I wish all of us luck, waving my arms like the parents of kindergarteners climbing onto a school bus. The world holds dangers, but we're bound to be ready to welcome those we sent forth home.

Housekeeping

Sleet falls over evergreens drooping with snow. I'm revising a manuscript that looks pretty familiar, which isn't a shock since I looked at it yesterday. And the day before, and the day before that. Then there's a moment of grace when I read, almost forgetting the words were first put down by me. But what if my satisfaction is complacency, stemming from the belief that I was done rather than from the scenes themselves? The dripping outside the windows gets too loud. My chest tightens as I survey syntax. I'm horrified by plump phrases I let slip by, and gratified for a chance to sweep them aside.

Sometimes the anticipation of being able to fill a vase with flowers and set it on a clean table helps get me through housekeeping. The neat-at-last stacks, the fluffed-for-once pillows, the afghan in its place bring pleasures like those of tinkering with punctuation. The past weeks have been devoted to such dust cloths, and I'm both happy and scared. The room is almost ready for guests I've longed to see. Then the nerves start wracking. What if I missed drifts of dog hair? What if this room where I've been cozy isn't a space where anyone else cares to sit? So I go back to tidying. A little bit necessary, a little bit obsessive. With my face near the floor, I might notice stains on the cabinets. One surface sends me to others. Just as I can never vanquish all signs of a dog in the house, I know I left sentences that one day I'll want to change.

Sometimes we have to bring in paperwhites or roses whether or not the tables got their long-promised shine. I finally reach a place in my manuscript where I find few words to change. Another round is finished. Then off it goes to Peter, who combs my manuscript for errant letters, missing articles, apostrophes doled out too randomly, the occasional *if* that should be *it*, or *she's* that need names. He puts gentle question marks beside poetic flights few will follow. His sweet manners on my pages make me smile with sentences such as, "It might be more clear if you had a verb in that sentence." Um, yes. And I'm glad for his occasional praise. "This may be the best description of a color I ever read."

I fixed everything I could, took a breath, and called the thing done.

Which gets a paragraph of its own. Still, when you "finish" writing a book (I can't even think "finish" without feeling my lips pucker to form quotes), there's a lovely sense of feeling one shoulders fall to more normal levels. Now I can make a loaf of banana bread, buy a new toothbrush, get my hair cut, hang out with my husband, repot the geraniums, bag books for the library book sale, read poetry, write poetry, climb a mountain, knit, wait, and try to refrain from obsessing about the status of my manuscripts in someone else's hands.

Or I can just rub my face with my hands. I'm determined to spend some time letting my thoughts drift toward an unborn novel, making myself available to the muse, who likes to find me on the window seat, looking unproductive.

I plan, but in a loose way, letting new ideas shuffle past the old, letting dusty ones drift away. I light a few squat white candles and let the small whispers of flames be music enough. A novel can be daunting – and I swear I'll never again write one as long as this last one – so I'm trying to trick my way in with a page here, a page there. I'm fooling around with characters, setting, and even action, spilling out scenes riddled with gaps. Like a bystander who's not terribly invested, I watch what will happen. Maybe just leaves blown aside. Maybe a book.

Writing reminds me that life isn't all beginnings and endings, but circles. Just as spring winds back to winter, finished goes back to not. My writing means lots of looping and splitting, moving back as much as forward, revising as I research, and researching as I revise. After staring down commas, I'm glad to be reckless again with punctuation, and even straightening my back and walking smack into mistakes. I put wrong words down on paper so I can find ones that might be right. Inconsistent characters? So what? Trying this, trying that, dropping things where they fall, then deleting whole passages.

Oh luddly beginnings – stop the spell check! Oh gimmers as well as glimmers of hope.

Saving Silence

The snow outside is a perfect four inches, covering the dried brown grass, but not daunting on the driveway. 'Tis the season of too much to do. I'm hosting a wreath-making party in a few days, have got a daughter who comes home soon, papers to grade, presents to be bought, wrapped, and mailed. There are cookies to bake, evergreen branches to hack down, and pine cones to gather. Sometimes the more other activities call, the more fiercely writing begs for my attention.

I become vigilant to protect silence against distractions from the upcoming holidays, the cat, and email that seems bound to be more charming than anything in my head. The kitchen is rarely perfectly quiet after the sun is all the way up. The phone might ring. Music might play. The dogs are at the window, determined to fend off squirrels marauding sunflower seeds meant for chickadees. Stillness can prickle, but if I sit it out, may turn benign instead of taunting. I may get a where-did-that-thought-come-from moment, feel a little wiser than my ordinary woman-in-the-kitchen-slicing-cucumbers-and-talking-on-the-phone self.

In December, solitude takes more effort to safeguard, though I also don't want to miss chances to see friends. So I went to a party the other night where three women told me about their struggles to hold onto some time of their own. There were stories of being asked to stuff envelopes, which led to the writing and signing of the letters being stuffed, which led to becoming chair of the PTO. One woman had begun a full-time job, so decided it was time to stop teaching her Sunday school class. To prep for this resignation, she wrote a script and pasted a sign saying "NO!" by the phone. Recapping this call, she told us she repeated, "No, I cannot do it," every other sentence. The other two women had long been co-organizers of a Christmas pageant. One said she called the secretary, explained that it was time for new input and creativity, then, after listening to some sobbing, said, "Well, maybe if absolutely nobody else can do it."

Uh, oh, we chorused. Yes, they were back to coaching the shepherds and wise men. One woman asked me how I turned down requests for help. They know I've got just one child who's living on her own and I teach just part time. This gives me time to write, an activity that's rather invisible to many people. I've learned that if I don't claim room for it, few others will, so I've practiced saying *No* without caveats or clauses and found the world keeps turning. Not that I'm entirely removed from the good work and friendships that volunteering can bring. I'm president of our local Friends of the Library, even if I just ended up there after I let myself be persuaded to take the slacker role of v.p., not foreseeing that our president would move out of town. But I won't accept a new responsibility until I've asked myself if I'm agreeing only because some old habits make *Yes* easier to say than *No,* until I've taken a hard look at what's the best use of the limited hours in a day. I try to make sure I don't agree to a task because it's easier than sticking with solitude, where second and third thoughts swoop.

Much as I like writing, there are some days when it just feels lonely. We need to make connections with living people and want an occasional short round of applause that writing seldom gives us. Most of us need some tasks with end results that we can see. Then we should get back to the silence where we sometimes feel as if we're pushing words with the energy it takes to drag a sled uphill, but are at last ready to ride, feeling the wind over our backs.

Words and Wreaths

Ever since our daughter was a baby, I've invited family and friends to our home to join us in making wreaths. I cut branches from the woods around the house and provide frames and decorations, a variety from earthy to frankly tacky. Guests bring cookies and help each other make bows. I get few chances for conversation as I move about adding armfuls of greens to the tables or pouring more punch in the bowl, but it's a visual treat to see the variety of wreaths. And after making sure clippers and green wire have been distributed, I make a wreath of my own.

A friend admired the bushiness of the one I made this year, the way branches jutted every which way. I told her that this was how I write, first going for broke, leaving the clipping for later. I let the colors of the spruce and hemlock suggest whether they want red ribbon, holly berries, pale dried grasses, or a glittery band of stars.

My friend worried that the stuff on her leaner wreath would blow away.

Peter, whose wreath was enormous, said, "That's what's supposed to happen."

The world is windy. Dried grasses or blooms fall off, like memories or extraneous facts. But the green circle holds for a while.

Ho Ho Ho! or Do You
Choose a Quiet Hum?

The tree is up. Our girl is home. Well, at least her stuff is. There are lots of, "Bye, Mom's," but we'll have her around for all of December 25. She has a talent I envy for finding gifts that are just right for their recipients. Peter spends much of the month prepping for the day and couldn't be more generous. I'm just pretty good at making snickerdoodles and thumbprint cookies.

I love the wave of family and friends I don't often see, the songs with lyrics I at least half-know, but I also savor quiet parts of the day. I'm up first on Christmas morning to feed the dogs the breakfast they eat every other day. I set out bread to rise and catch a few minutes of reading by the tree, my elbow by an angel with chipped wings made by my Grandmère long ago.

Soon my in-laws and our friends Pat and Ed arrive with presents and pies. My brother-in-law, Bruce, walks from sunroom to kitchen, camera in hand, and tries to get a shot of the chickadees and brilliant cardinals at the feeder.

"They're so fast," he says. "Pete, how do you get those pictures?"

Peter explains that his camera has a special setting for quick movement. He sits for about ten minutes watching to get the rhythm of particular birds, to know when they'll take flight, when they'll land. Then he tries to match their timing.

Yes, a bird metaphor is coming. And I expect this one has been made before, but I'm flying forward because the words remind me of quietly watching how characters behave in their daily lives, then diving for words when something ordinary suggests a moment that might be revelatory. I imagine characters going on their rounds just as I do: there's breakfast, procrastination, and snow to sweep off steps. Sometimes I hear a real broom's sound and know it can be of use on paper. But today I return to the oven, and set out silverware and plates. My father-in-law says grace. Peter cracks jokes at the end of the table across from me, laughing with our beautiful daughter. The green beans with dried cranberries aren't too hard or too soft and there is only one comment about the missing mashed potatoes. The dogs share the ham bone. Between the dining room and the kitchen, while clearing dishes, Pat, whose recent scans haven't been good, hugs me hard and says, "I might not have another Christmas, but I have this one."

We cry a moment, then set out star cookies and pie.

Three

A friend recently complained to me about a copy editor who'd deleted or changed words on her manuscript that she'd intentionally used several times. She marked many with "stet," which means those original words or phrases should stay where they are. Sometimes we inattentively repeat, especially when we're patching together parts, but other times we consciously want words to bring readers back to a color, fragrance, or quirk of speech. Poetry runs with this concept with the refrain. The same line at the end of every stanza may add music, and at its best, faintly underscores what comes ahead or behind. Echoed sounds help shape everything, reminding us that a frame doesn't have to be just on the outside.

Repetition can stamp something into memory. The power of its rhythms may help readers see something new, though we don't want to go on and on and on (should I have stopped with one or two *on's?*). Repeated things or places may also give readers a sense of control through having things temporarily patterned.

Most work involves repetition, too. When I bake a cake, I start with a list of ingredients and a particular kitchen counter. Someone who builds a house can't just be in love with the vision of new walls, but must work nail by nail and board by board. Those trying to cure cancer must take long hard looks at slides of cells for days and years on end. Monks and nuns count beads or footsteps through a labyrinth. The cake, house, cure, and salvation can be kept in mind, but it's good if people like working with sifters, measuring tapes, microscopes, rosaries, or words until, if we're lucky, the marvelous appears.

But how much is too much? Three is a good number to keep in mind. It's no accident that it often appears in fairy tales with bears, beans, spins around, or wishes. Three objects, speakers, or illustrations often appear on a first page, giving a satisfying sense of symmetry, while remaining more dynamic than the sleepier pattern of two by two.

Three good examples tend to be stronger than a slew, and have been chosen for little kittens, billy goats gruff, stooges, trilogies, the trinity, wise men, sky-land-and-sea, triumvirates, musketeers, and Fates. Martin Scorsese is said to have called the dream movie scene one with three people in a room. And there's narrative itself, based on beginnings, middles, and ends that shift into each other. All good scenes, and even many good sentences, may include first, an event, second, the way characters react to what happens, and third, a hint of why what happened matters. Triangles can have the enduring nature of circles, while being less cozy. They suggest something could spring or spill.

A Candle in the Writing Room

The world outside is snowy. Inside, the oranges in the wooden bowl are getting soft. The cookies are stale. Evergreen needles are scattered on the floor. Peter hacked apart the tree, hauled the limbs out the door, and stashed the trunk with others in the garage. You never know when you might need a stripped balsam trunk, I suppose. Emily and a friend confer on the computer among scraps of ribbon and the edges of clipped photos, remnants of a project.

It's the season of new calendars and resolutions, which seem bound to be kicked aside by Martin Luther King Day. Themes for the new year seem more possible, but even they don't sound like something I need. I figured I'd forget the whole renewal notion. Work isn't going so badly, meaning I'm writing, even through an emotionally taxing week. Then, searching for a book on my shelf, I put my hand on one I wasn't looking for, but which I thought would move a friend who shares my concern about Pat, whose latest round of chemo mixes has turned as ultimately ineffective as the others, and whose doctor says experimental treatment is her only choice now. I knew this book wouldn't make our sorrow any less, but it was still worth giving and reading. Flipping through the poems, I realized that rough, inexact beauty often keeps me moving forward in hard times.

So here's my simple plan -- and I don't have to count words, hours, anything. I'm going to move slowly forward with a manuscript that won't be finished until I can make it as beautiful as I feel the subject deserves. Each day I mean to nudge a page or paragraph to be more elegant, tender, or spacious. I'll write or delete until I can celebrate a few words that fit my own definition of beauty, an awkward kind, the way we may feel bearing chocolate or flowers into an over-decorated hospital room, knowing what's in our hands won't be enough.

My goal is to add something that wakes up my eyes and holds the focus between me and my screen. This is not about "you must," but about rewards that are smack in the middle of the process. I'm approaching the task like the form of meditation I sometimes do -- gentle, western, undemanding: when thoughts stray, I just quietly move back and start again. Some days all I might manage of beauty is moving a not-quite-there sentence up to one that's finished. Or deciding that a scene whose potential I can gauge is triumph enough.

I'm forgoing new vows and schedules, and lighting a candle as a reminder of what flickers, warms, or casts a shadow as I try to see the whole. There's a scrap of paper by my elbow, with a phone number reminding me of another visit to set up, and how I must listen in order to know what Pat needs, as well as being the person who's clueless about what to say. There's illness and too much snow, but also friendship and somewhere singing, and another cardinal at the bird feeder.

A New Year

Pat wore her angel necklace to the clinic where she's getting experimental treatment. I sat beside her, wearing the bracelet she'd given me with blue beads and a cherub at the clasp and boots that got slush-stained in the parking lot. She drank what could technically be called gunk in preparation for a scan. The nurse said this thick drink is pina colada flavored, but it's got to be vile. Pat sipped through a straw with a parasol that a friend had given her. It's a sweet gift, and I love Pat for, among other things, the way she tries to make every occasion festive. But as I sat beside her in an ugly plastic chair, I wished I weren't expected to smile. The results shown on the scan might be bad or worse, and we were braced to be grateful for bad.

We writers for children are expected to be advocates of hope and happy endings. So are teachers like Pat, who's taught special ed or reading for more than thirty years. She can imagine triumphant endings for her students, and has the gift of being able to see one bit of time for itself. Lately, this means she can say that she had a rough morning, or afternoon, or sometime day, but she doesn't talk about difficult weeks and months. This amazes me.

On our drive to the university clinic, she told that she still prays for a miracle. I want the miracle I know she envisions, too. But while I believe anything can happen, all the writing I do, trying to arrange events in a believable order, makes me suspicious of out-of-the-blue salvation. Writers are lucky that we get to end things where we choose on a page, but I feel the strain of optimism, the tendency to charade, while sitting in molded plastic chairs with boots dripping all around. Watching people come and go, I wondered, *Who's sick? Who's sicker? Who's best at coping? Why can't the clinic supply better magazines?* There's always hope, but I need to acknowledge its different shades: what seems reliable, what's cheap, what's zig-zagging, and what looks more like anger.

I don't plan on marching into darkness, but there's

strength to be found by looking straight ahead at what seems true. I'll always find traces of joy woven through sorrow, just as I can spot beauty even on bleak days. I'm happy to have a smart, healthy girl and loving husband, two good-natured dogs, a cat who's mean but sometimes sleeps on my feet, new students to meet soon, a yoga class, and good friends. I have all the words I can use. But I want to know the difference between the smiles I give because someone may need them and the smiles that happen on their own. I want to see what I see with my own eyes and claim my own views, while remaining a supportive friend. To take in the whole landscape -- the stars, but also the dark sky around them.

I said none of this to Pat, but after I drove her back home, and promised that I'd pray while she waited for results, I thought of the ways plots change as children move from picture books to the grittier novels for teens, where not every ending is happy and some stories are grim all the way through. But are they appropriate for the young? Absolutely. And do they offer hope, that bounding, boundary-pushing willingness to be startled, to find humor or beauty where we don't expect it? Almost always, found in the message that even when we feel alone, we aren't entirely. Any book can remind us that readers, writers, and characters are all in this together.

Horizon

A few days later, Pat called with the test results. Her first words were, "Good news, Jeannine! It hasn't spread to my liver."

Looking on the bright side is Pat all the way, and I realized those who've spent their lives looking for silver linings may well spend the last chapters of their lives that way, too. And why not? With so much else out of control, we humans get to shape our life stories, or at least decide what we want to claim as a climax. We get to set a tone.

"Let's go to Maine for the weekend," I suggested.

We booked a room where I ate room service lobster salad and she stuck to crackers, then curled into our beds with books. Emily called, and we enjoyed passing the phone back and forth. The next morning, we brought muffins and tea to the beach. Pat's the sort of person who when the weather is thirty degrees but sunny thinks it's a great beach day, and it is.

We met an older couple walking along the rocks who told us they thought they'd spotted a whale.

Pat squealed.

The man said, "It's moving kind of fast on the surface."

His wife replied, "A whale is my story and I'm sticking to it."

But it was kind of fast, kind of on the surface, and after a while we all conceded it was a boat.

After all my questioning of what I thought of as Pat's too sturdy hope, I missed it. After telling myself that I was prepared for the worst, I wasn't. Late in February, soon after Pat was told her quick-spreading cancer made her no longer eligible for more experimental treatments, she checked into the hospital. We're not sure when she'll get out.

Emily flew in from LA. She sits to my right as we

drive, the way she did when I picked her up from middle school and told her that a friend who'd been another mom in our baby playgroup had died that morning. Emily wailed, which marked a particular bend in Route 5 forever in my mind. She sits beside me as I drive the way we had when going to see her Uncle Don for what would be the last time, just a few years ago. I'm proud that she took the time and found the strength for that trip and this one. I wish she didn't have to.

I steer between broken rock on either side of the highway, over hidden rock that must join the cliffs. Emily reaches over, lifts a strand of my hair, then lets it drop. We look at each other.

Not long ago Pat said, "I might not get one more Christmas, but I have this one." We might not get another day with Pat, but soon the three of us talked about everyday things, while wondering if we'd ever get another chance to be within the circle of each other. There's so much we can't know. But we have this day, and it matters.

Intruders at the Laptop

"Is there a way to write without risking crying at the computer?"

I was just asked this by a thoughtful graduate student embarking on a complicated writing project, and who would rather not do this by a box of tissues. I told her, "Not really, but it will be all right."

As a student, she doesn't know many details of my life, though I offer glimpses between the edges of the curriculum. All of us come to our writing with lives, even if we're not taking them on as subjects, and so hers is a reasonable question. I mentioned that some people can compose anything without feeling overwhelmed. Journalists have to contend with catastrophes all the time, and I expect some of those writing novels showing the world at its worst may construct dystopias while eating a sandwich. But I find that sitting quietly can leave me open to all sorts of moods. Sadness, which caregivers may neglect during days of making an effort to look bright for other people, may snatch this chance for attention. Sorrow may swoop across the writing desk, just as it might when a song comes on the radio while we're driving to get groceries, or in the darkness when our heads nestle on pillows.

Some of us begin writing from personal history. Others find it creeping into the middle of the process, even if we don't end there. Memory may spill into cracks, though it shouldn't limit our choices or dictate fiction's structure. And when we write about anything, we tap into our mind without discriminating much between what's true or imagined, what happened first or last. In early drafts it's best if we can welcome everything, rather than trying to swat some parts away. If we find sadness sharing the chair, if tears come, they do so for a reason and aren't the worst thing we'll ever know. Fears need to be feared and disappointments need to disappoint. Dashed hopes rarely get swept up as quickly as they were broken.

I write to ease loneliness and connect with others, and

that won't happen unless I tell the truth. While I like to hear and give good news as much as anyone, life hands out more than trophies and cake. We shouldn't emphasize the bad any more than we should color the world entirely in rainbow hues. It's good to be where we are and to see what we see. We don't need to tell everyone we encounter about our trials, but we need to commune with ourselves as honestly as we can.

Cardinals

Pat was very weak by the time she settled into her bedroom. I was among the bevy of women who with her husband, Ed, kept her company, prepared food she might be able to keep down, washed and hung sheets, answered the phone, and tracked down soothing music. We tried to make sure that two or three people were in the house, one to be with her, and one stationed in the kitchen to let visitors in and out.

I often set my laptop on the kitchen counter, and sometimes after showing people to Pat's bedroom, came back to write. Not on any of my projects, but simply to put down what I was seeing, hearing, or feeling. I remembered reading that Henry James took notes at a funeral, claiming that writers are people on whom nothing is lost. I agree with that last part, but always hated that story. I don't want to be Henry James, but I had to do something. I don't pray in a diligent way, unless prayer is navigating the tightrope of all I know and don't know, rather than implorations such as *Please let her get well* or *Thy will be done,* which I'm not in the mood for. I was too distracted to read and there were only so many dishes to be washed, and our friend, Sue, was quick to tidy the counters. Writing some of what I witnessed helped me to sit still when I felt on the edge of tears. It was a way to look for broken beauty as winter ended and spring returned.

I heard Pat laugh the day before she closed her eyes and stopped talking. On the third day that she slept with no signs of awareness, I sat in the kitchen with a business card from a mortuary near my hands. Ed, who we'd been begging to take a break, had handed this to me just before he left to take a motorcycle ride, saying that I should call them if Pat … He ended his sentence with her name.

I looked out the window and watched two cardinals peck seeds. The brighter male fed one seed at a time to the female. Their beaks touched. Moments later, a friend tiptoed in from Pat's bedroom. I knew Rosemary would leave Pat for only one reason.

Rosemary, Sue, and I went to the bedroom, where we listened to Pat not breathe. I made the call. I heard a motorcycle. I stepped into the garage and looked at Ed, who'd been so very briefly gone, after months and years of caring for his wife. We hugged, and he said, "I knew it would happen like this. The hospice nurse said she was probably holding on for me."

None of us wanted this day to come, but if it had to, and I suppose it did, everything happened about the way Pat had wanted. We'd taken turns that morning whispering to her phrases we hoped would be a comfort, though none of us knew what, if anything, she heard. The cherry tree was almost in bloom. Soon a few more friends arrived and we wandered up the country road or around the yard, crying, then coming back to each other for hugs or to pat the big white dog. We went inside and stood around the dining room table, which was piled with papers, and talked about a service. There was nothing to do now, not what we'd all wanted to do, and yet we were about to be called into motion to get a funeral in order. This meant choosing poems, music, pictures, and who would say what. And trying to believe that even words that someone might call sentimental, sappy, or imprecise were perfect. Because they were chosen and were what we had.

Crossing Back to Work

In the past few days I spotted two bears in the woods, helped run a library program, filled vases with lilacs, planted pansies a friend gave me, read two remarkable theses and listened to students defend them. I turned in grades. I heard the phone ring a few times and thought: It's not Pat. I got briefly cheered up reading a packet of letters sent from a school where I'd talked about writing, including one from a boy who began: *I love your book so mush.*

Trying to work on my novel, I shove and shuffle words around. I tell Peter that it's hard to get back.

"Does it feel trivial?" he asks.

No. There's the good news. I suppose my women from history could look irrelevant, but I see something there. It's just hard to give fiction the focus it needs. Grief, like a brown toad squatting on rotting leaves, surprises. Sometimes I feel on top of sadness. I'm old enough to have been through the deaths of loved ones before, which must count for something. Other times, well, too early one morning I let loose at a telemarketer. "I can't find my glasses, the dogs are barking, and ... my friend died." I burst into sobs.

"I'm sorry, ma'am. Should I take you off the list?"

"Yes! We're already supposed to be off!"

Perhaps this time did the trick.

I'm doing okay, but am not what I've come to feel familiar with as "myself." Sometimes I see the sun and a bowl of strawberries on the porch table, the dogs sleepy at my feet, my husband doing his morning's reading, and I think how these are good things. Life, as they tell you, does its going on thing.

But today I wished I had a reason to put on teacher-ish clothes, or at least someone had a big project to send me. Teachers can open windows, then move on, and I'm often grateful for tasks that soothe with some predictable elements, a curriculum to follow. It can be harder to take out white paper, which may reflect what we're trying to evade. Even if we've taken on subjects seemingly far from our lives, or moved forward within outlines with known characters and agendas, at some point we face thoughts and feelings that don't fit into the boundaries of our work. Mourning, like life, sets its own schedule. Memories spiral, offering revelations with each re-telling, or burrow in. They may lead to places dim as the early drafts of my fiction. Such murkiness doesn't rise just because we can't find the right tone or structures, but mirrors our minds, which pull in all that we don't know and can overwhelm what seems certain.

Once again, I open my novel, grateful it's there waiting for me, hoping something will snag my attention. But first I write in my journal, feeling sad writing about Pat, but closer to her, too. I've written many pages about our almost daily phone calls, including her observations on treatments and side effects, reports on doctors and nurses, determined affirmations, worries for her husband, anger at her sisters, grief for her dead parents, and gratitude for friends. I write the way someone might keep accounts of sins, blessings, calories, or miles walked, writing for a purpose apart from making something lovely with language. This and my own worries were the weather in my head, what I batted through to get to other stories and set old characters in new motion.

Tucked behind grief and thoughts of spotted bananas and how good bread would smell, I notice, the way we do when revising a story, an object in the corner that might stand for a whole life. Though it has nothing to do with the work I intended for the day. Or does it? The wandering mind is also the creative mind. Letting thoughts stray may make new connections. We might need to dwell in what's uncomfortable, trying not to swat off sadness or even kindness in an effort to hold onto a world that has changed. We should respect both everyday time and ritualized time, when we may fit what's common into bigger patterns.

And there's a moment to rein in meandering thoughts, and no clock to announce when to use a little force to separate old plans from new mayhem. Just as sensitive friends try to figure out how much quiet and how much company the bereaved might need, we try to figure out how much we should sit with sadness and how much we need our feet on what we guess is normal ground. I slowly turn my mind back to my characters.

At last, and this is brief, I smile at a sentence, and tell my writer-self: Yes. Thank you very mush.

Old Quilts

One day when browsing in an antique shop, I found a small stack of colorful old patches that someone had painstakingly sewn, but never bound together for a quilt. After buying them, I called a seamstress friend for advice, found new fabric for a backing and borders, then stitched away. As I worked, I noticed that the old fabric pulled. As I kept on, full-fledged rips appeared.

I mentioned this to my seamstress friend. Now she said, "Oh, yeah, that would happen. The new stitching will stress the old cloth. But anyway, it's about the process."

Um, no, I thought. I wanted something to put on a bed. But sometimes the process is what we get. Sore hands, soft curses over the sewing machine, and a quilt that's pretty though left folded and untouched, lest it tear some more. We write stories we thought might make someone laugh, blink away tears, or stand straighter, but instead they stay in our rooms. Was the process of looking carefully at what's under our hands or in complicated pasts worthwhile? I think back to being a child and playing games that had finishing lines. I'm certain now that the playing, friends, and family were more important than who won or lost what.

We're not the grownups we thought grownups were back when we were children. We're more confused. We keep making mistakes. We learn that some things we thought were possible aren't, and that some things we believed were impossible are possible after all. We don't all write stories to preserve the past, and we don't all stitch old squares into new patterns. Some of us are hugely ambitious and some of us are glad for a small audience. Many of us strive to balance a drive to keep going with the ability to cherish where we are.

Stitching together those old quilt squares, I was trying to complete something beautiful that someone else had put away for reasons I'll never know. I'm sorry that the quilt was unraveling even before I unplugged my sewing machine, that an unknown woman's work didn't get a second chance. I'm not looking for neglected projects under any more tables at antique shops, but I won't stop looking for unfinished stories. Like people who've worked with cloth or yarn through the centuries, almost always without their names attached to their work, we can't know what part of what we leave behind will matter. Some of us keep pricking our fingers, making stitches whether or not they hold.

Last and First Words

Words aren't people, but the right ones may make us feel as glad as we do when almost colliding into an old friend at the grocery store. Words aren't things, but some shine like a clasp that musically snaps open or closed. Finding the right words can make us feel as if we belong just where we are. And we can change our world, or at least our impression of it, by deciding what to name what we see. For instance, when Emily last came home, she noted, "The cat is getting fat."

"He doesn't run about the way he used to. Maybe he's putting on a little weight."

"Fat," she said.

Then when I took him to the v-e-t today – his second scheduled appointment as, despite our sneaky efforts like spelling out the destination, he managed to elude both me and my husband on the first one – the vet asked if there were any problems.

"No. Maybe he's getting more sluggish," I said.

"Laid back," she corrected me.

Which does sound better. So when the Zen cat drapes himself across the sofa top, I'll try to be reminded of the value of relaxation. And that words make a difference. Names may call up more than the things themselves, wrapping them in the history of language. The apple on a table is likely to be a snack, but on paper it might suggest Eve reaching for a fruit tree or Snow White dipping her hand into a peddler's basket. A rose is a rose, but the word calls up all the ways it's been used before.

Abstract words, such as justice or humanity, seem to belong in offices or universities with few pictures on the walls. Concrete nouns or verbs that show off muscle seem at home in kindergartens, carrying associations as sturdy and particular as crayon stubs and construction paper kept in cubbies. Small words may be as layered as peeling wallpaper, catching old conversations or vanished stories. I reach for those with Anglo-Saxon roots over the Latinate, not that I've studied that old language from Rome, but I can recognize pomp or puffiness, a drift away from particular tables, toads, or toenails. Words derived from Anglo-Saxon, unencumbered by prefixes and suffixes, often keep closer to a mental picture. Lyrics of an old song set "Show me the way to go home" against "Indicate the way to my habitual abode," contrasting the language of someone with two feet firmly on the ground with a stereotype of a stuffy scholar. George Orwell points out more examples of words that seem intended to obscure if not deceive in his essay, *Politics and the English Language.*

Of course as soon as we set down a rule, we might stand it on its head. An abstract word may be just the thing in the right specific surroundings, perhaps chosen to soften or lull instead of slam, or point to an unusual horizon. Nouns and verbs are often gorgeously strong and spare, but sometimes an adjective or adverb, such as the one I just put in front of "strong," may let us see more clearly or change the rhythm. Used with discretion, adjectives can beam some extra light, but it's wise to avoid overused pairings such as a blue sky, a red apple, a bouncing ball, a crying baby, or a pretty girl. Readers are more likely to see the sky in their minds' eyes if it's called purple or yellow, though we don't have to get fanciful. Colors are usually better than qualifiers that evaluate, but it can be still better to move from what we can see to what we can hear, smell, or feel, citing a ragged hem rather than a blue dress, or a sleeve falling in slick not yellow butter. Description may move beyond the moment to hint at a connection, say if a mother writes on a green felt blotter, while her daughter swings, maybe several pages later, a green butterfly net. Really, the only rule is to pay attention.

Into the World

I write because thinking and moving my hands at the same time bring me more clarity than using my mind alone. Writing feels like the water I'm meant to swim in, though the related duties and gifts of publication can shift the current. During the first few weeks after I'd sent my book about Enheduanna to the editor who'd asked for a revision, I daydreamed about when and where she'd open the file. As weeks turned to months, I wondered if she was sharing the manuscript with others in the office before she got back to me. My notion of a possible fall release in a year and a half shifted. Maybe spring publication would be better.

At last I got an email with the title *Conversations with the Moon* in the subject column. I raced through praise for the language and a nod to the subject's importance. My eye stopped on the word "but," which was followed by the observation that my previous book had not sold particularly well. The editor was sorry. So was I. I'd thought that four starred reviews and several best-of-the-year lists for *Borrowed Names* counted enough so that I'd get a chance to publish another book, but I was wrong. I wrote a polite note thanking the editor for her time.

It takes a while to rally, but the response to any rejection is to write more and better. Keeping on the path helps me keep believing that I have a chance, though my chances don't look the way I dreamed back when I started dreaming. When I get a rejection letter for a manuscript I won't imminently revise, I make a point to send it out again by the next day. Then I get back to writing, teaching, spending time with my family and friends, and trying not to count the days since sending off my manuscript. Eventually, I heard from another editor, who wrote that she was glad to learn about Enheduanna, but didn't see how publishing a book about someone few people have heard of could make much money. And her name is hard to say and spell.

Okay, but couldn't we try our best? Here is the first

person known to have taken written language beyond lists and laws. She gives us a look into a time when writing was powerful and mysterious, and another view of a land that we know about mostly because of soldiers on its soil. I sent out a few more queries and got back to waiting. I still haven't heard from some editors who know me in various ways, which makes me feel like I'm walking through a building where I was told I'd find colleagues, but no one says hello.

Silences stretching through seasons hurt, but I remind myself there may be reasons I'll never know, and some the cost of having small publishers bought by large ones. I haven't given up on getting Enheduanna's story into the hands of more readers, thought the business is such that anything I send out may have its potential sales measured against those of my last published book. *Borrowed Names* earned out its advance, went into a second printing, and sold about five thousand copies more than *Goodnight, Moon* did during the first year that it was published. Not that my book of poems is much like that picture book with its great green room, but I bring it up because for about ten years, *Goodnight, Moon* left shelves in un-astonishing numbers, until slowly sweeping up toward its present status as a standard at baby showers, with sheets and pillow cases to match. It came out when a book was given time to find an audience. Those are not our times.

Publishers have always meant to make money, but they once relied on slower ways of passing along information. Sales now can be counted within minutes or days, instead of months or years, and while word of mouth remains important, we get the sense that those words should be loud and quick. The business has changed since I was the undergraduate being told by a professor that I had what it took, if I could withstand uncertainties. Back then, many believed that it might take some time, but eventually good work would find a home. I can't tell my students that now. I remember when books deemed more commercial than literary were published with the thought that the money that bestsellers made would enable the publication of books that wouldn't sell a lot, but would mean a lot to a few people. Editors stood behind authors while an audience was built. Now many buy books in the hope that they might become the next bestseller, and even authors whose books sell briskly may be cut from lists if their newest book doesn't move beyond the sales of their last one.

Trends change. Luck shifts. Justice prevails, sometimes. Such thoughts have kept youthful hope alive in aging me, holding out for the one editor who might believe my work will sell enough to make publishing it worthwhile. And for the book now in your hands, I'm being my own advocate. I've been told that independent publishing is the recourse of the thin-skinned, or those with terrific marketing skills, or those whose writing isn't strong enough to pass muster with traditional publishers. Since I no longer believe that good work is bound to find a place, I have to also question my old ideas about independent publishing, and let go of my outdated wish for a stamp of approval on my work. Oh, that longing for someone to say, "This is good, and I can help you make it better," is still there. I've worked with wonderful editors, some of whom still help usher out wonderful books, and I miss them.

But those who make judgments based on sales predictions are not people I should be seeking affirmation from. I recall examples of independent publishing success that I'd considered exceptions. Virginia and Leonard Woolf set up their own imprint, following in the footsteps of the Bronte sisters. Charlotte reports publishing a collection of poems that sold two copies, but "Ill-success failed to crush us: the mere effort to succeed had given a wonderful zest to existence: it must be pursued." Much closer to home, Peter has been urging me to self-publish for decades, for it's a path he took with a comic book he wrote and drew with a friend. That first comic book led to a series that swiftly became so popular that when I was struggling to get my high school students to appreciate Shakespeare or Willa Cather, more than one teen asked how I could be so much less cool than my husband. This would not be the last time I heard this question. It followed me long after sales of *Teenage Mutant Ninja Turtles* meant I could stop teaching, have a baby, stay home with our child, and write.

Changing technology means I can self-publish a book for less money than Peter and his friend Kevin borrowed and invested about thirty years ago, and print-on-demand means we don't have to stack cartons and padded envelopes in the dining room because of the need to buy in bulk. I'll make decisions on fonts, page size, covers, pricing, and many other things, and if people don't like my choices, I have only myself to blame. There will be typos, and worse. Eek! And, oh well. I've learned to live with other mistakes along the way.

One of my pleasures in writing this book was that I didn't have to wonder about who would publish it. I would. Starting small, standing up for myself, seeing what happens. Sometimes it's fun and sometimes I feel like an athlete who swapped teams and found herself sitting on the bench. She might start her own team, though she's not thrilled to hunt down teammates, locate equipment, and keep all the balls and fences in shape. But she'd rather play on a field whose borders aren't well marked than not play at all.

Publishing isn't entirely different than writing. I try to be brave, but my stomach sometimes feels tied in knots. I often work alone, but friends aren't so far away. I'd hoped I'd left behind taking cash and checks when I left a job I'd held at a stationary store to become a teacher. I'll do my best to at least earn back my expenses, but when talk turns toward fortunes to be made by independent publishing, I find I'm needed in another room. I don't want to hear the Amazing Success stories. I cheer for those who've made it big, or even achieved justice – like that of romance writers who are popular but paid a pittance, and can now earn closer to what they deserve. But tales of great triumphs scare me. I don't want to spend more time on publishing than I do writing, so it seems wisest to keep my expectations small. I mean to remember Charlotte, Emily, and Anne Bronte, and exult if I sell more than two copies.

Maybe I won't be so bad at this. I'll consider Stone Door Press a success if logistics don't become overwhelming, if I don't do anything too embarrassing, and if a few people are inspired by my words. I've learned from each editor who has helped guide my other books into print and under covers. I'm thankful to have had books published by two great small presses. Lee and Low and Dawn Publications have kept my books in print for many years. My editor for five books at Farrar, Straus and Giroux, who's no longer in the business, sooner but mostly later passed along reviews, casually shrugging both at praise and qualifiers, saying, "We like the book."

That small, sweet *we* made it easy to move on from whatever others said. Such confined expectations sound a little quaint, though historically it wasn't so long ago when I began publishing, which was before the Internet was widely used. This meant that while I didn't yet know the good company I'd find on listserves and among bloggers, and I didn't have easy access to lots of information about publishing, I had only a vague sense of awards within my field. Now I can learn not only the dates when some major prizes are given, but can find results in seconds, which somehow makes them feel more important. I can distract myself by compulsively checking for reviews, for which there are ever-increasing outlets. More written opinions may be good for marketing, but bad for an author's tendency to obsess, procrastinate, and look back instead of at the empty pages we should be filling.

Some people choose to self-publish reasoning that since they do a lot of the marketing anyway, they should get paid more for their time. That makes sense, but I'm drawn to this route because I hope to bring back the feeling that I can write a book, shepherd it quietly into the world, and go on to create something new. I can gauge its worth using the measure of my own heart, which was shaped partly in a small church in a small town. I'm a long way from being the child who climbed steep stairs to the choir loft, put on a blue robe over my Sunday-best dress, then lifted my hair so another girl could fasten the hook and eye at the back of the rounded collar. But I remember watching Mr. Brown, a cheerful man who also drove the school bus, pulling so hard on a rope that his heels lifted from the ground as the bell pealed.

Don't we all want to use all our strength and concentration, then let go, while a sound makes a way into the world?

At Last

Inspiration doesn't come to us as much as we come to inspiration. The world is always waiting. And time slips as I write about a present that shuffles back even as I try to hold it in words, reaching for an ending. All writers must decide what last gift to leave before closing one book and finding a way into another.

Because I've published books for children, I'm sometimes asked to visit classrooms where I may talk about what I do, then pass out paper. Recently, I asked a class of third-graders to write about a favorite place. I walked between rows reading over shoulders about tree houses, backyard forts, bedrooms, a nook in a dad's apartment. One girl who couldn't wait for me to reach her desk hurried over, tapped my am, and handed me a paper about her father's gravesite. How I wanted to hug her. Or go home and take a nap. I said, "That's a nice detail about the yellow dandelions."

As she smiled, my mind spun with worries about a wedding without a dad, household bills, and whether a stepfather was in the picture and what he was like. I said, "It's good you remembered the five senses. Maybe you could say something about how the flowers smelled or if you picked one, how it felt under your chin."

She raced off with her paper, sneakers squeaking, elbows bobbing, while I stopped at the next desk. When my allotted half-hour was over, I crossed the hall to the fourth grade, where I asked the students to write about a hero. One boy gave me a description of his little sister who'd worn his baseball cap through chemotherapy treatments. I wondered whether his sister was still sick or even alive. I kept myself from asking how he managed to get up and put on socks and shoes each morning. I didn't even say, "I'm sorry," because the offer of sympathy may seem like a request for it. I didn't ask, "Are you all right?" for no truthful answer would be simple. Instead I asked, "Do you want to put in something that you said to each other? Do you know how to make quotation marks?"

I leave you with the ordinary and magnificent courage of children who trust their hearts to paper, then go on to tackle math exercises, or skip rope, or unroll brown bags holding sandwiches. There I am, walking up and down aisles, saying, "Keep going. Give me more details," which may mean, "People want to know. They will be as brave as you are, though it might take time to see. Tell the truth about what you remember."

Every small thing matters. Don't forget to look.

Acknowledgements

I thank and love my husband and our daughter for many reasons, but among them is the way Peter and Emily Laird, along with our extended family, never question that writing is part of my life. My critique group -- Bruce Carson, Dina Friedman, and Lisa Kleinholz -- have improved every book I've written. This one began as entries from my *Views from a Window Seat* blog at http://jeannineatkinsonwritingandstuff.wordpress.com. In its online archives, you can find some variations of what's here, many entries that aren't included, photographs, and comments from others, which show how online conversations enrich and shape ideas. I'm grateful for exchanges with friends including Susan Hoyle Bailey, Susan Taylor Brown, Nancy Castaldo, Debbi Michiko Florence, Jen Groff, Laura Hamor, Sara Lewis Holmes, Irene Latham, Becky Levine, Kerry Madden, Jenny Moss, Kelly Ramsdell, Candice Ransom, Jama Rattigan, Melodye Shore, Tara Smith, Toby Speed, and Lorraine Meray Thomas.

This book depicts times with good friends, but I cut some names since there seemed too many for one book. I'm glad for the beautiful lives of Pat Cook, Ed Smith, Mary Shanley-Koeber, Sue Weeks, Karen Lederer, Margaret Arsenault, Jess Berget, Bruce Laird, and my second grade writer buddies, Heather Ramsey and Naomi Sohlman. Among the treasured writer-friends whose presences stand behind some pronouns here are David Costello, Peg Davol, Erin Dionne, Cynthia Faughnan, Amy Butler Greenfield, Jo Knowles, Michelle Kwasney, Sarah Lamstein, Marjorie Light, Cynthia Lord, Kate Messner, Burleigh Muten, Deb Paulsen, Nancy Hope Wilson, and Ellen Wittlinger.

Cherished Books about Writing

None of us really work alone. My list of books that taught me about craft and made me want to write better starts with *Bird by Bird: Some Instructions on Writing and Life* by Anne Lamott, which is full of wisdom and humor. Lovers of imagery should read *The Left-Handed Story: Writing and the Writer's Life* by Nancy Willard. The title of *Art and Fear* by David Bayles and Ted Orland can sound intimidating, but it's filled with great tales, like that of a ceramics teacher who divided his class into those who'd be graded on the quantity of pots they made and those who would get an A for making a single excellent pot. Guess which side did best? Hint: It's always about the work.

I've mentioned E.M. Forester, and think his *Aspects of the Novel* is essential. Edith Wharton's slim volume, *The Writing of Fiction,* offers advice from one of its masters. I often refer to C. S. Lewis's thoughts, and his "Three Ways on Writing for Children" is an important essay that can be found online. And Laura Miller is my favorite author about C.S. Lewis. *The Magician's Book: A Skeptic's Adventures in Narnia* offers an elegant reflection on the ways that books we read as children can change within us as we age.

Just as there are too many friends to mention here, there are too many helpful books to cite. In other words, there will be times when I'll cringe at the thought of who and what I've left out. One more reminder that writing means finishing one thing and going on to the next, even while thinking that what came before was not quite good enough. Or maybe it was. Some things aren't for us to say.